"Who Do You Say That I Am?"

120 Questions and Answers About Jesus Christ

by James J. Drummey

C.R. PUBLICATIONS INC.
345 PROSPECT STREET
NORWOOD, MASSACHUSETTS 02062

C.R. Publications Inc.
345 Prospect Street
Norwood, MA 02062
www.crpublications.com

Second Printing October 2009

Cover by Ariel Design
Printed in the United States of America

ISBN 0-9776099-2-8

CONTENTS

PREFACE

Of all the questions that have been asked about Jesus, He Himself asked the most important one of all: "Who do you say that I am?" For the way in which one answers this question could determine one's fate for all eternity.

Was Jesus just a good man who went around preaching love of God and neighbor? Was He just a religious leader, like Buddha or Confucius? Was He just another prophet in the line of biblical prophets, one who stirred up people for a while and then was put to death? Or was He, as Simon Peter said, "the Messiah, the Son of the living God"?

This book attempts to answer those questions by delving into exactly what Jesus said and did during His time on earth. The Gospels of Matthew, Mark, Luke, and John remain the most reliable sources of information about Jesus, and the reader of this book must consult those sources often, as well as some of the works cited in the bibliography.

While any opinions expressed in this book are entirely those of the author, I wish to express gratitude to those who read the manuscript and offered helpful suggestions. This includes Msgr. Paul J. Hayes and Elizabeth M. Drummey. Many thanks also to Fr. Albert H. Stankard, whose wonderful portrait of Christ appears on the front cover, and to Patrick Madrid for writing the Foreword.

If everyone's eternal destiny depends on their accepting Jesus as the way, and the truth, and the life - and it does - then the more one knows about Him, the better are one's chances of getting to Heaven. If this book can assist in that journey, it will have been worth the effort.

James J. Drummey
September 14, 2008
Feast of the Exaltation of the Holy Cross

FOREWORD

Imagine this: The year is A.D. 30. The place is Caesarea Philippi, a town in northeastern Israel. You find yourself standing near twelve men who are grouped around and conversing intently with their leader, Jesus Christ. You are about to witness a momentous episode in Christ's three-year public ministry.

He asks the Apostles two questions. First, "Who do men say that the Son of Man is?" This elicits a variety of answers: "Some say John the Baptist," is one reply. "Others say Elijah, and others Jeremiah or one of the prophets," says another. The voices trail off into silence. After a few moments, Christ asks them, "But who do *you* say that I am?"

These twelve men, the Apostles, are the Lord's closest friends and hand-picked collaborators. They have lived and traveled with Him for the past two years. They have watched, over and over again, in dumbfounded amazement, as He performed countless miracles and astounding deeds: healing the sick, raising the dead, multiplying a few morsels of bread and fish to feed over 5,000 people, casting out devils, calming the wind and the waves of a storm with one word of command, reading the secret thoughts of men and women, walking on water.

One would think that these men, above all others, would have a very clear idea about Jesus' identity. And yet, they fall silent. All of them, that is, except the brash fisherman Simon, who declares, "You are the Messiah, the Son of the living God." To which Jesus responds: "Blessed are you, Simon Bar-Jona! For flesh and blood has not revealed this to you, but my Father who is in heaven" (Matthew 16:13-17).

What you have just witnessed is the moment when Christ clearly and unambiguously confirmed His identity as the Messiah, the Son of God. And from this truth, which God the Father revealed to Simon Peter, the entire gospel of Jesus flows. It is His identity as *true God and true man* (cf. John 1:1-14) that is the foundation for everything He said and did, everything He taught His disciples, and everything He commanded them to preach and teach in His name, henceforth until the end of the world (cf. Matthew 28:19-20).

Christ's identity as the God-Man is the key to understanding His message. Without knowing who He is, one simply cannot understand, much less enter deeply into, the glorious mysteries of His gospel. And this is why a book like *"Who Do You Say That I Am?"* can be so useful for so many.

For example, millions of contemporary Catholics, who have not been the beneficiaries of a solid and comprehensive catechesis, and therefore are at best hazy in their understanding of who Jesus Christ is. Millions more, who find themselves outside the Catholic Church, have deficient and often even woefully defective understandings of Jesus Christ. They don't really know who He is. It would be a major understatement to say that this is a serious problem.

Contradictory and erroneous opinions about the identity of Jesus Christ are widely promoted and thus cause widespread spiritual damage to people who are contaminated by them. As Scripture reminds us in 2 Peter 3:16, some people "twist Scripture to their own destruction." And I can think of no better, kinder, more charitable thing one can do than to help someone else avoid the spiritual ruin which can result from misunderstanding what Scripture means by what it says about who Jesus Christ really is.

And that's where this book comes in. In it you will encounter a wide and illuminating array of scriptural truths about who Jesus Christ really is, the testimony of early Church Fathers, the teachings of the popes and councils and saints over the centuries. Reading this book will help you be able to say with clarity and conviction, along with Simon Peter, "You are the Messiah, the Son of the living God!" This is the firm and joyful conviction that should shine forth from every Catholic today, just as it radiated from all those many men, women, and children who, down through the centuries, have suffered the supreme sacrifice of martyrdom for their unswerving fidelity to Christ and their belief in His divinity.

The more deeply you immerse yourself in the mystery of the Incarnation of Jesus Christ, the Second Person of the Blessed Trinity, the Word who became flesh and dwelt among us, the more firmly you believe it, and the more willingly and boldly you proclaim it, the more prepared you will be to meet Him face-to-face and be happy with Him forever in eternity.

Patrick Madrid
Feast of All Souls, 2008

Chapter 1

The Historical Jesus

Q. How do we know that Jesus is a real historical figure?

A. No figure has made a greater impact on human history than Jesus Christ. The year in which we live is measured from the date of His birth. More than two billion people throughout the world call themselves followers of Christ. Tens of thousands of books have been written about His life and teachings, and He has been the subject of numerous films, musicals, and documentaries.

The existence of Jesus is attested to by such first-century non-Christian writers as the Jewish historian Flavius Josephus and the Roman authors Pliny the Younger, Tacitus, and Suetonius. But the most reliable and detailed sources of information about Christ are the four Gospels written by Matthew, Mark, Luke, and John, men who either knew Jesus personally or talked with those who knew Him.

In a negative vein, Jesus is the only person in human history whose name is used to express anger, surprise, and disgust. The name of Julius Caesar, the famous Roman general and statesman who died only a few decades before Christ was born, is never used today in a profane manner. Nor is the name of any other ancient or contemporary person used in such a crude way.

"Jesus is no myth," said Pope Benedict XVI in his book *Jesus of Nazareth*. "He is a man of flesh and blood and he stands as a fully real part of history. We can go to the very places where he himself went. We can hear his words through his witnesses. He died and he is risen" (pp. 271-272).

It was an unknown author, however, who provided a most striking summary of Jesus' life and His effect on history in these words:

"Here was a man born in an obscure village, the child of a peasant woman. He grew up in another obscure village. He worked in a carpenter shop till He was thirty and then for three years He was an itinerant preacher. He never wrote a book. He never held an office. He never owned a home. He never traveled two hundred miles from the place where He was born. He never did one of the things that usually accompanies greatness.

"While still a young man, the tide of public opinion turned against Him. His friends ran away. One of them betrayed Him. Another denied he ever knew Him. He was turned over to His enemies. He went through the mockery of a trial. He was nailed to a cross between two thieves. While He was dying, His executioners gambled for the only piece of property He had on earth and that was His tunic. When He was taken down, He was laid in a borrowed grave through the pity of a friend.

"Nineteen wide centuries have come and gone and today He is still the centerpiece of the human race and the leader of the column of true progress. I am far within the mark when I say that all the armies that ever marched, and all the navies that ever sailed, all the parliaments that ever sat, and all the kings that ever reigned, put together have not affected the life of man upon this earth as powerfully as this one solitary life."

Q. How is Jesus different from such famous religious leaders as Buddha, Confucius, and Mohammed?

A. Archbishop Fulton J. Sheen said that Jesus is different in three ways: First, He is the only person in history whose coming was pre-announced. No one predicted the birth of Buddha in 563 B.C., or Confucius in 551 B.C., or Mohammed in 570 A.D. But the biography of Jesus was written hundreds of years before He was born, notably in the Old Testament writings of such prophets as Isaiah, Micah, and Zechariah.

Even the Roman historian Tacitus, a pagan, wrote that "people were generally persuaded in the faith of the ancient prophecies, that the East was to prevail, and that from Judea was to come the Master and Ruler of the world."

Second, once Jesus appeared, He divided all history into two periods, the one before His coming (B.C.) and the other after it (A.D.). Even those who deny Jesus, said Archbishop Sheen in his *Life of Christ*, must date their attacks upon Him, A.D. so and so, or so many years after His coming.

Third, said Sheen, while every other person who ever came into this world came into it to live, Jesus "came into it to die. Death was a stumbling block to Socrates - it interrupted his teaching. But to Christ, death was the goal and the fulfillment of his life, the goal that he was seeking. Few of his words or actions are intelligible without reference to his cross. He presented himself as a Savior rather than merely as a Teacher" (p. 4).

Or as John said in his Gospel: "For God so loved the world that he gave his only Son, so that everyone who believes in him might not perish but might have eternal life" (John 3:16).

Furthermore, while neither Buddha nor Confucius ever claimed to be more than ordinary human beings, Christ claimed to be God and demanded the allegiance of all humanity. There is no comparison between His divine Personality and the ordinary human personalities of Buddha and Confucius. It could never be said of them what John the Evangelist said of Jesus in the fourth Gospel: "In the beginning was the Word,/ and the Word was with God,/ and the Word was God./ ... And the Word became flesh/ and made his dwelling among us" (John 1:1, 14).

Q. You said that the Gospels give us accurate information about Jesus, but how do we know that the Gospels are reliable history books?

A. We know that the Gospels are reliable historical works because we know when they were written and who wrote them, that their authors were well informed about Jesus, that they could not have deceived us about Him even if they wanted to, and that these four books are substantially the same today as when they were written. Let's look at each of those statements individually.

When were they written? Although no publication date appears on the Gospels, we know from scholarly investigation that they were composed in the last half of the first century, between 50 and 100 A.D., or about 20 to 70 years after the events reported in them. We can determine when the events in the life of Christ occurred by comparing them with contemporary events and secular rulers. For example, the Gospels tell us that Jesus was born when Caesar Augustus was emperor of Rome, Quirinius was governor of Syria, and Herod the Great was king in Judea.

We also know from the Gospels that when Jesus began His public life some 30 years later, it was "in the fifteenth year of the reign of Tiberius Caesar, when Pontius Pilate was governor of Judea, and Herod was tetrarch of Galilee, and his brother Philip tetrarch of the region of Ituraea and Trachonitis, and Lysanius was tetrarch of Abilene, during the high priesthood of Annas and Caiaphas" (Luke 3:1-2).

Who wrote them? Tradition has identified the authors of the Gospels as Matthew, Mark, Luke, and John. This tradition is affirmed by St. Irenaeus of Lyons, who died around the year 200. Writing in a work entitled *Against Heresies*, Irenaeus, a pupil of St. Polycarp, who had known John the Apostle, one of the evangelists in question, wrote the following:

> "Matthew also issued among the Hebrews a written Gospel in their own language, while Peter and Paul were evangelizing in Rome and laying the foundation

of the Church. After their departure, Mark, the disciple and interpreter of Peter, also handed down to us in writing what had been preached by Peter. Luke also, the companion of Paul, set down in a book the Gospel preached by him. Afterwards, John, the disciple of the Lord who reclined at his bosom, also published a Gospel, while he was residing at Ephesus in Asia."

Were the authors well informed? Yes. Matthew and John were Apostles of Christ and were with Him all during His public life. Mark was a secretary or companion of Peter, the leader of the Apostles, and wrote down what Peter said. Luke was a secretary or companion of Paul and a careful historian who compiled "a narrative of the events that have been fulfilled among us, just as those who were eyewitnesses from the beginning and ministers of the word have handed them down to us" (Luke 1:1-2).

Could the authors have deceived us? Matthew, Mark, Luke, and John had nothing to gain by writing what they did. They were not praised or celebrated, but were rather persecuted and even put to death for telling the truth about Jesus. People might be ready to lay down their lives for the truth, as the Apostles did, but not for a lie. Even those who crucified Christ did not accuse the evangelists of lying, for the truth was too well known.

Furthermore, they could not possibly have been guilty of deception. What they were relating had been seen by thousands of people, many of whom were still alive when the Gospels were first preached and then written down. Certainly the enemies of Christ would have leaped at the chance to expose any falsehoods in the four Gospels.

There were other "gospels" written in the second and third centuries that resembled the New Testament in subject matter and title, for example, "gospels" attributed to Peter, Thomas, and Mary Magdalene, but these writings were so lacking in historical accuracy that the Church rejected their authenticity.

Are the four Gospels that we have today substantially the same as when they were written? We say *substantially* because there are minor differences in certain insignificant words due to the human frailty of those who copied the Gospels by hand before printing was invented in 1450. But scholarly study of the thousands of manuscripts in existence confirms that the copies of the Gospels that we have today are substantially the same as when they were written in the first century.

Their accuracy can also be confirmed by comparing them with the writings of non-Christian historians at that time and by reviewing the many archaeological diggings that have occurred over the centuries. Those explorations have corroborated down to the smallest details places and events described in the Gospels. "One has to visit Palestine," said travel writer H.V. Morton in his book *In the Steps of the Master,* "to understand how meticulously accurate is the Bible" (p. 171). Morton found that he could read pertinent passages from the Gospels while visiting Jacob's Well or the Inn of the Good Samaritan or the Garden of Gethsemane and feel that he had been transported back to the time of Christ, so accurately did the evangelists describe those places.

Therefore, we can safely say that the Gospels are reliable history books and that what they tell us about Jesus is true.

Q. Do the Gospels tell us everything about Jesus?

A. No, but they tell us as much as we need to know to follow Jesus. At the end of his Gospel, John said that there were many other things that Jesus did during His public life, but remarked that if he tried to include them all, there would not be enough books in the whole world to contain them (cf. John 21:25). John did not mean this literally, of course, but it is an indication that many things were left out. For example, we know nothing about the first thirty years of Jesus' life, except for His birth and the time He was lost in the Temple at the age of twelve.

The Gospels, by the way, are not four separate books, but really just one Gospel with four versions. One needs to read all four to get the whole story about Jesus. For example, we know that Jesus spoke seven times from the Cross, but Matthew and Mark record only one saying ("My God, my God, why have you forsaken me?"). There are three other sayings in Luke and three more in John.

Q. Do we know the exact year in which Jesus was born?

A. No, we do not. In the sixth century, a monk named Dionysius Exiguus drew up a calendar that fixed the birth of Christ in the Roman year 753, but scholars today agree that Dionysius miscalculated by a few years. So it is probable that Jesus was born four or five years before the usually accepted year 1 of the Christian era.

Q. Instead of using B.C. (Before Christ) and A.D. (*anno Domini* - in the year of our Lord) in calculating time, some people use B.C.E. (Before the Common Era) and C.E. (Common Era). What should Catholics do?

A. Catholics should remember that even time has a Christological significance, and they should use the traditional vocabulary of B.C. and A.D., which is part of our common language of faith. Jewish scholars, who not surprisingly were uncomfortable with these abbreviations because these scholars did not recognize Jesus as the Messiah, began using the designations B.C.E. and C.E. Catholics and other Christians, however, should keep Jesus at the center of salvation history.

Q. We call our Lord Jesus Christ, but wouldn't it be more accurate to call Him Jesus the Christ?

A. Yes, it would be more correct to call Jesus "the Christ" since **"Christ"** in Greek (and **"Messiah"** in Hebrew) means the "anointed one" and is a title for our Lord, not His last name. Jesus was anointed by the Holy Spirit and sent into the world by the Father to bring about our Redemption. His name in Hebrew means "God saves," and that is why we also call Him **"Savior,"** but there is nothing wrong with calling Him Jesus, or Christ, or Jesus Christ, or Christ Jesus since from ancient times all these names have been properly used for our Lord.

In his book *Jesus of Nazareth*, Pope Benedict XVI explained that the title Christ "quickly ceased to function as a title and was joined with the name of Jesus: Jesus Christ. What began as an interpretation ended up as a name, and therein lies a deeper message: He is completely one with his office; his task and his person are totally inseparable from each other. It was thus right for his task to become a part of his name" (p. 319).

Q. Why did Jesus call Himself "Son of Man"?

A. This appellation, which appears 80 times in the Gospels, is a title Jesus used to indicate His messianic mission of bringing salvation to the world and His role as judge at the end of time. "Whoever is ashamed of me and of my words in this faithless and sinful generation," said Jesus on one occasion, "the **Son of Man** will be ashamed of when he comes in his Father's glory with the holy angels" (Mark 8:38). The title also emphasizes the humanity of Jesus just as "Son of God" emphasizes His divinity.

One of the most striking uses of the title appears in chapter 7 of the Book of Daniel (7:10, 13-14), where the prophet had a vision of God sitting on His throne and being ministered to by "thousands upon thousands" and "myriads upon myriads" of angels. As the visions continued, Daniel said, "I saw/ One like a son of man coming,/ on the clouds of heaven;/ When he reached the Ancient One/ and was presented before him,/ He received dominion, glory, and kingship;/ nations and peoples of every language serve him./ His dominion is an/ everlasting dominion/ that shall not be taken away,/ his kingship shall not/ be destroyed."

It was Jesus' repetition of these words in the early morning hours of Good Friday that so infuriated the Sanhedrin and led to His being condemned for blasphemy. For when the high priest Caiaphas asked Him if He were the Messiah, the son of the Blessed One, Christ replied, "I am;/ and 'you will see the Son of Man/ seated at the right hand of the Power/ and coming with the clouds of heaven' " (Mark 14:62).

Q. What does it mean to refer to Jesus as the "new Adam"?

A. One way to see the connection between the two major sections of the Bible is the process known as **typology**, whereby certain persons, events, or things in the Old Testament prefigure or foreshadow persons, events, or things in the New Testament. Thus, Adam is a type of Jesus, who is called the "new Adam." For as St. Paul explained, just as through the one person of Adam sin entered the world, and was followed by death, so, too, grace and justification came into the world through the one person of Jesus Christ. In conclusion, said Paul, "just as through one transgression condemnation came upon all, so through one righteous act acquittal and life came to all" (Romans 5:18).

Q. What do the letters "IHS" mean?

A. While some have said that the letters come from the Latin *Iesus Hominum Salvator* ("Jesus, Savior of Man"), Patrick Madrid offered this answer in *Envoy* magazine: "IHS is the anglicized rendering of the first three Greek letters in Jesus' name. In the early Church, especially during the time of Roman persecution, this became a popular way of writing Jesus' name as a sort of code. Since then, it has become a universally used insignia and shows up on all kinds of Catholic religious art and accouterments" (*Envoy*, February 2008, p. 58).

Q. There is a Bible commentary which says that "critical scholarship" has cast doubt on the Christian belief that the Book of Isaiah makes predictions about Christ. What do you say?

A. We say that the "critical scholars" are wrong, for the Church has always insisted that Isaiah referred to Jesus in several places. For example, there is the **Immanuel prophecy** where Isaiah said: "Therefore the Lord himself will give you this sign: the virgin shall be with child, and bear a son, and shall name him Immanuel" (Isaiah 7:14).

And then there are the famous passages that refer to the sufferings of Jesus. These **"Servant Songs"** can be found in chapters 42, 49, 50, 52, and 53 of Isaiah. Consider just the following verses and try to imagine them referring to anyone but Jesus:

> "Yet it was our infirmities that/ he bore,/ our sufferings that he endured,/ While we thought of him as stricken,/ as one smitten by God/ and afflicted./ But he was pierced for our offenses,/ crushed for our sins,/ Upon him was the chastisement/ that makes us whole,/ by his stripes we were healed" (Isaiah 53:4-5).

Chapter 2

Jesus: True God and True Man

Q. How is Jesus true God and true man? Did He shed His divinity when He came to earth?

A. No, He did not shed His divinity when He came to earth. He is true God and true man because there are united in His divine Person, without any confused mixture of both, His divine nature and a human nature. In the words of the Council of Chalcedon, which was held in 451, Jesus is "one and the same Son, our Lord Jesus Christ, perfect in his humanity, true God and true man, composed of rational soul and body, consubstantial with the Father by his divinity, and consubstantial with us by his humanity, 'like us in all things but sin' (Hebrews 4:15), begotten from the Father before all ages as to his divinity, and in these last days, for us and for our salvation, born of Mary, the Virgin and Mother of God, as to his humanity."

We call the unity of the two distinct natures of Jesus in the one Person of Christ the **hypostatic union**, and the fact that the Son of God assumed a human nature and became man in order to bring about our salvation the **Incarnation.** Jesus is not part God and part man but truly God and truly man.

Q. Has this doctrine of the two natures of Jesus in one Person been disputed in the history of the Church?

A. Many times. Major heresies arose in the early centuries of the Church that denied at least one aspect of this doctrine, and councils were called at places like Nicaea and Ephesus to oppose these heresies For example, there was the heresy of **Gnostic Docetism,** which denied the humanity of Christ and taught that He only seemed to be a man. There was **Arianism**, which denied the divinity of Christ and regarded Him only as a superior creature and intermediary between God and the world. There was **Nestorianism**, which denied the real union of the divine and human natures in Christ and taught that while Mary could be called the Mother of Christ as man, she could not be called the Mother of God. There was **Monophysitism**, which held that Christ possessed only a divine nature. And there was **Adoptionism**, which taught that Christ was the Son of God not by nature but by adoption.

Even in our own day, there are those who question the divinity of Jesus. In response to them, the Vatican's Sacred Congregation for the Doctrine of the Faith issued in 1972 a declaration on "Errors Concerning the Mysteries of the Incarnation and the Trinity" *(Mysterium Filii Dei)*. This declaration said that those who view Jesus merely as a divinely inspired human being "are far removed from true belief in Christ, even when they maintain that the special presence of God in Jesus results in his being the supreme and final expression of Divine Revelation."

Q. Why was the Incarnation necessary? Why did Jesus become man?
A. The Incarnation was necessary because Adam and Eve had committed an infinite offense against God. No mere human being could make up for that offense. The people of the Old Testament tried to do so through sacrifices of animals and crops, but they were unsuccessful. It was only when God, the Second Person of the Blessed Trinity, took on a human nature that atonement for the sin of Adam was possible. As God, Jesus could offer infinite reparation to His Father for the offense; as man, He could take the place of sinful humanity and save us from our sins.

In summary, the *Catechism of the Catholic Church* (nn. 457-460) says that the Word became flesh in order *"to save us by reconciling us with God,"* so that *"we might know God's love,"* so that Jesus could become *"our model of holiness,"* and so that He could make us *"partakers of the divine nature"* [2 *Pet* 1:4].

Q. Can you explain the relationship of Jesus to the Father and the Holy Spirit in the Blessed Trinity?

A. The Trinity is the central mystery of our Catholic Faith and the source of all the other mysteries. It was Jesus Himself who revealed to us that there is one God in three divine Persons: God the Father, God the Son, and God the Holy Spirit. It is beyond human understanding how there can be three Persons, but only one God, but we accept this teaching because it was revealed to us by Jesus, who is Truth itself and can neither deceive or be deceived.

When we make the Sign of the Cross, we make it in the name, not the names, of the Father and of the Son and of the Holy Spirit, for there is only one God in the **Most Holy Trinity.** All three Persons are equally God - the Father is completely God, the Son is completely God, and the Holy Spirit is completely God. While they are distinct from each other, they are united in one nature. Thus, it would be wrong to say or to imply that only the Father is God, for the Son and the Spirit are one and equal with the Father. The three divine Persons do not share the one divinity among themselves; each of them is God whole and entire.

Q. If Jesus is equal to the Father, then why did He say, "I am going to the Father; for the Father is greater than I" (John 14:28)?

A. When Jesus speaks in His humanity, He can say that the Father is greater, but when He speaks in His divinity, as when He said, "The Father and I are one" (John 10:30), He is stating His equality with the Father. Since Christ is both God and man at the same time, He is equal to the Father in His divinity, and less than the Father in His humanity. Jesus was made man in such a way that He never ceased to be God and, since He is one Person, He used the personal pronoun "I" whether referring to His divinity or to His humanity.

Q. If God the Son is equal to God the Father, why does the Son have to act as mediator between me and the Father? Why can't He act on His own?

A. Jesus is given the title mediator because He reconciled God and humanity. This title comes from 1 Timothy 2:5-6, where St. Paul says: "For there is one God./ There is also one mediator/ between God and the/ human race,/ Christ Jesus, himself human,/ who gave himself as ransom for all." Here is how Fr. John Hardon explained the title in his *Modern Catholic Dictionary:*

> "Christ is best qualified to be the mediator, i.e., one who brings estranged parties to agreement. As God, he was the one with whom the human race was to be reconciled; as a human being, he represented the ones who needed reconciliation. Christ continues his work of mediation, no longer to merit the grace of human forgiveness, but to communicate the grace already won on the Cross."

Q. Can you point out some places in the Gospels where Jesus claimed to be God?

A. There was the time in the synagogue at Nazareth when Jesus read a prophecy from Isaiah about the Messiah and then told His listeners that the passage from Isaiah was fulfilled in their presence (cf. Luke 4:21). He was claiming to be the promised Messiah.

There was His conversation with the Samaritan woman, who said that she knew that the Messiah, the Anointed One, was coming, and Jesus told her that He was that Messiah(cf. John 4:25-26).

On another occasion, He told the disciples, "Everyone who acknowledges me before others I will acknowledge before my heavenly Father" (Matthew 10:32).

Or the time when He said, "The Father and I are one," and His listeners picked up rocks to stone Him. "I have shown you many good works from my Father," Jesus said. "For which of these are you trying to stone me?" The Jews answered him, "We are not stoning you for a good work but for blasphemy. You, a man, are making yourself God" (John 10:30-33).

And of course at His trial before the Sanhedrin just hours before His death, Jesus was asked by the high priest Caiaphas, "Are you the Messiah, the son of the Blessed One?" Our Lord, knowing that His words would mean certain death, replied: "I am" (Mark 14:61-62). Caiaphas tore his garments and accused Christ of **blasphemy**, of claiming to be God, and the Sanhedrin condemned Him to death.

Q. We know that Jesus claimed to be God, but can we prove that He is God?

A. If Jesus claimed to be God and He was not God, then He was either a liar or a lunatic. But there is nothing in the accounts of His life as recorded by Matthew, Mark, Luke, and John that would even suggest that He was untruthful or that He was crazy. The Gospels make clear that Jesus was a Person of outstanding character and exemplary virtue. He was a quick-witted and spellbinding speaker, a compelling storyteller, a great moral teacher, and a wise and compassionate spiritual leader. He was the perfect man.

So if Jesus was not a liar or a lunatic, as C.S. Lewis said many years ago, then He must have been Lord and God. His divinity can be demonstrated first by the Old Testament prophecies that He fulfilled, second by the prophecies of the future that He made, and third by the dozens of miracles that He performed.

In the first category, Jesus is the only Person in history whose biography was written hundreds of years before He was born. He and only He fulfilled scores of Old Testament prophecies about the Messiah who was to come. He was descended from the House of David (Isaiah 11:1), born in Bethlehem

(Micah 5:1) of a virgin mother (Isaiah 7:14), worshiped by kings bearing gifts (Psalm 72:10), betrayed (Psalm 41:10) for 30 pieces of silver (Zechariah 11:12-13), and "pierced for our offenses,/ crushed for our sins" (Isaiah 53:5).

Second, Jesus was able to predict the future Himself, something that only God can do with certainty. Not only did Christ predict the various things that would happen to Him during His Passion, and that He would rise from the dead, He also foretold the destruction of Jerusalem (Luke 21:24), which took place forty years later, in A.D. 70.

Third, since miracles are by definition beyond the power of science and nature, and can only be explained by the power of God, the fact that Jesus performed dozens of them during His brief public life demonstrates that He is God. He called these miracles His divine credentials and said that these works would confirm the fact that His Father had sent Him (cf. John 5:36). Recall that many of these miracles were witnessed by crowds of people and that even Jesus' enemies could not deny what they saw with their own eyes. Their response to the raising of Lazarus from the dead, for example, was to condemn the Lord for performing this miracle on the Sabbath and to initiate a plot to kill Him and Lazarus, too (cf. John 11:53, 12:10).

The Gospels provide us with plenty of convincing evidence that Jesus was just who He claimed to be.

Q. But aren't there people today who deny that Jesus performed miracles, or who say that His works were not miracles at all?

A. Yes, there are such people, but their credibility is undermined not only by the overwhelming evidence for miracles in the Gospels, but also by the fact that even the enemies of Jesus testified to His wondrous works. "What are we going to do?" the Pharisees asked. "This man is performing many signs. If we leave him alone, all will believe in him" (John 11:47-48).

As for those who say that miracles are scientifically impossible, we say that science is the study of physical laws and cannot prove that those laws can never be overridden. If human beings can override the law of gravity by pumping water uphill, why can't the One who created these laws override them?

What is a **miracle**? It is a visible event that is outside the course of nature and can only be explained by the power of God. Jesus said that if people didn't believe His words, then perhaps they would believe the spectacular works that He performed. For example, there were His miracles of nature, where He walked on water, twice produced large catches of fish, and calmed the wind and the waves.

There were His miracles of sustenance, where He changed water into wine at a wedding feast and where He multiplied five loaves of bread and two fish to feed more than 5,000 people. This was a real miracle, not a case of inviting people to share their own food with each other.

There were His miracles of healing, where He gave sight to the blind, hearing to the deaf, mobility to those who were crippled, healthy flesh to those afflicted with leprosy, and even life to three persons who had died, including His friend Lazarus, who had been dead for four days (cf. John 11:1-44). This miracle was witnessed by scores of people, and there were two reactions to it. One group was more convinced that Jesus was God and continued to follow Him; the other group decided that Jesus was a threat to them and initiated a plot to kill Him.

There were miracles of exorcism, where Jesus cast out devils. Recall the time that He sent the demons into a herd of swine, who rushed down a hill and drowned in the sea (cf. Mark 5:1-20).

But Jesus' greatest miracle of all was His Resurrection on the third day after His brutal death on the cross. The enemies of our Lord couldn't deny that the tomb was empty on Easter morning, so they paid the soldiers who had been guarding the tomb to spread the story that the Apostles had stolen the body of Jesus while the soldiers were sleeping. What they could not explain away, however, were the more than 500 eyewitnesses who said that they saw Jesus in the forty days after the Resurrection. St. Paul indicated how important this miracle was when he said that if Jesus did not rise from the dead, our whole religion is a waste of time (cf. 1 Corinthians 15:14).

Q. Why did Jesus perform miracles?

A. For several reasons: to show the power of God to alleviate suffering, to invite people to believe in Him, to prove His divinity, and to testify to some truth or to confirm some teaching (the multiplication of the loaves and fishes prefigured the doctrine of the Eucharist and the raising of Lazarus foreshadowed Jesus' Resurrection and our own).

Q. How do we answer statements in modern works of fiction, such as *The Da Vinci Code*, that no one knew Jesus was God until the Council of Nicaea (in 325) declared by "a relatively close vote" that He was God?

A. We point out that Jesus is described as God or as God's Son more than 100 times in the New Testament. For example, when the Apostle Thomas was invited by Jesus after the Resurrection to put his fingers into Christ's wounds, Thomas fell to his knees and said, "My Lord and my God!" (John 20:28).

Furthermore, many saints testified that Jesus was God long before the Council of Nicaea, such as St. Ignatius of Antioch, who in 107 referred to "our God, Jesus Christ," and St. Justin Martyr, who in 150 said that Jesus was "God, Son of the only, unbegotten, unutterable God."

As for "a relatively close vote" at Nicaea, the bishops at that Council already knew that Jesus was God, but wanted to make clear that He was equal to the Father because a lot of Catholics were being led astray by a priest named Arius, who said that Jesus was the highest of God's creatures, but he was not fully God. So the bishops voted (218 to 2) to affirm that Jesus was true God and equal to the Father. They approved the Nicene Creed that we say every Sunday at Mass, that Jesus is "God from God, Light from Light, true God from true God, begotten, not made, one in being with the Father."

Q. But what about the claim that Jesus was married to Mary Magdalene?

A. There is no evidence anywhere, not in the Gospels of Matthew, Mark, Luke, and John and not even in the phony "gospels" promoted by those who believe this falsehood that Jesus and Mary Magdalene were married. The usual evidence cited is this passage from the Gnostic Gospel of Philip: "And the companion of the Savior is Mary Magdalene. Christ loved her more than all the disciples and used to kiss her often on her mouth."

Not only does this say nothing about marriage, but here is how the passage appears in the original manuscript, which has many holes in it: "... the companion of the [...] Mary Magdalene. [...] loved her more than [...] the disciples, and used to kiss her [...] on her [...]." Fill in the blanks any way you want, but they offer no evidence that Jesus and Magdalene were married.

Q. Did Jesus always know that He was God, or did He only gradually become aware of His divinity and His mission on earth?

A. It is the teaching of the Catholic Church that Jesus, because He was a divine Person with both a divine nature and a human nature, knew of His divinity and His mission from the beginning. Jesus had two kinds of knowledge - human and divine, and three kinds of human knowledge:

(1) He had the **Beatific Vision**, which is an immediate face-to-face knowledge of God (He knew that He and the Father were one). (2) He had infused supernatural knowledge, which was knowledge conferred on Him by God without previous human experience or reflection on His part (He was able to read the hidden thoughts of His listeners and could predict future events). (3) He had acquired knowledge (He learned how to read and write and become a carpenter).

In his *Question and Answer Catholic Catechism*, Fr. John Hardon offered this summary of Christ's knowledge:

> "Christ, as God, knew all things, past, present, and future. And even as man, because His humanity was united to the Word of God, He had access to all knowledge; but since the nature He assumed was finite, His human knowledge was not infinite. Therefore, He could develop as man through the kind of experience He had as He grew from infancy, through childhood, and into adult age. But never was Christ ignorant of anything He could have known, as though He were not God-made-man from the first moment of the Incarnation; or ignorant of anything He should have known, as though His human nature was blinded, like ours, by original or personal sin" (pp. 64-65).

We also have the statement of Pope John Paul II that Jesus first proclaimed His Messiahship publicly in the Temple at the age of twelve when He told Mary and Joseph, "Did you not know that I must be in my Father's house?" (Luke 2:49). This response, said John Paul, was our Lord's "manifestation of his awareness that he was the 'Son of God' and thus of his duty to be 'in his Father's house,' the Temple, to 'take care of his Father's business' (according to another translation of the Gospel phrase). Thus Jesus publicly declared, perhaps for the first time, his Messiahship and his divine identity."

For more information about Christ's knowledge, see paragraphs 472-474 of the *Catechism of the Catholic Church* and Fr. William G. Most's book, *The Consciousness of Christ*.

Q. But didn't Jesus say in the Bible that only the Father knows when the end of the world will come? Since Jesus is God, wouldn't He know this information as well?

A. The passage about the end times to which you are referring can be found in Mark 13:30-32, where Jesus said, "Amen, I say to you, this generation will not pass away until all these things have taken place. Heaven and earth will pass away, but my words will not pass away. But of that day or hour, no one knows, neither the angels in heaven, nor the Son, but only the Father."

It is natural to think that Jesus, as the Son of God, would also know when the world was to end but, as the *Catechism* explains, He was not sent by the Father to make that information known. It was not proper for Him as man to reveal that part of the message. In the words of the *Catechism* (n. 474):

> "By its union to the divine wisdom in the person of the Word incarnate, Christ enjoyed in his human knowledge the fullness of the understanding of the eternal plans he had come to reveal [cf. *Mk* 8:31; 9:31; 10:33-34; 14:18-20, 26-30]. What he admitted to not knowing in this area, he elsewhere declared himself not sent to reveal [cf. *Mk* 13:32; *Acts* 1:7]."

Q. In the film *The Last Temptation of Christ*, Jesus is shown as being subject to sinful passions and desires. Was it ever possible for Him to sin?

A. No, it was never possible for Jesus to commit a sin because it would have meant that God was capable of sinning against Himself. Since Christ was a divine Person, whose every act was an act of God, He could not sin. "In him there is no sin" (1 John 3:5), says John the Evangelist. And the author of Hebrews says, "For we do not have a high priest who is unable to sympathize with our weaknesses, but one who has similarly been tested in every way, yet without sin" (Hebrews 4:15).

When we are tempted, our will wavers and we find ourselves leaning toward evil. There was no wavering will in Christ, no inclination toward sin, and no struggle in choosing between good and evil. Jesus had both a human will and a divine will, but as the Third Council of Constantinople (680-681) taught, His human will followed His divine will "without resistance or reluctance."

Why did Jesus subject Himself to temptations (cf. Matthew 4:1-11 and Luke 22:39-46)? Perhaps to show us how to overcome them in our own lives. "Because he himself was tested through what he suffered," says the Letter to the Hebrews (2:18), "he is able to help those who are being tested."

Q. If Jesus was sinless, why was He baptized by John?

A. Jesus was indeed sinless and had no need of baptism, but He submitted to John's baptism, over the objections of the Baptist, to show that He was accepting and beginning His mission of salvation as God's suffering servant. Jesus was allowing Himself to be numbered among sinners and to be seen as the Lamb of God who takes away the sin of the world (cf. John 1:29). He was anticipating a baptism of blood on the cross, in perfect submission to the Father's will, and consenting to die for the remission of our sins.

In *Jesus of Nazareth* (p. 18), Pope Benedict XVI explains the significance of this event:

"Looking at the events in the light of the Cross and

Resurrection, the Christian people realized what happened: Jesus loaded the burden of all mankind's guilt upon his shoulders; he bore it down into the depths of the Jordan. He inaugurated his public activity by stepping into the place of sinners. His inaugural gesture is an anticipation of the Cross. He is, as it were, the true Jonah who said to the crew of the ship, 'Take me and throw me into the sea' (Jon 1:12).

"The whole significance of Jesus' Baptism, the fact that he bears 'all righteousness,' first comes to light on the Cross: The Baptism is an acceptance of death for the sins of humanity, and the voice that calls out 'This is my beloved Son' over the baptismal waters is an anticipatory reference to the Resurrection. This also explains why, in his own discourses, Jesus uses the word *baptism* to refer to his death (cf. Mk 10:38; Lk 12:50)."

Q. In Luke 18:19, our Lord asked the rich official why he called Him good since only God is good. This is confusing since Jesus Himself is God.

A. Yes, <u>we</u> know that Jesus is God and that He is good, but the rich official did not know this, so Jesus' first step was to point the man in the direction of God. As Pope John Paul II explained in *Veritatis Splendor*, in order to answer the official's other question ("Good teacher, what must I do to inherit eternal life?"), Jesus first noted that eternal life "can only be found by turning one's mind and heart to the 'One' who is good: 'No one is good but God alone' (Mark 10:18; cf. Luke 18:19). *Only God can answer the question about what is good because he is the Good itself."*

The Holy Father explained further that "the goodness that attracts and at the same time obliges man has its source in God, and indeed is God himself. God alone is worthy of being loved 'with all one's heart, and with all one's soul, and with all one's mind' (Matthew 22:37). He is the source of man's happiness. Jesus brings the question about morally good action back to its religious foundations, to the acknowledgement of God, who alone is goodness, fullness of life, the final end of human activity, and perfect happiness" (n. 9).

Q. A professor in Florida has stated that Jesus didn't walk on water; He really walked on ice after the Sea of Galilee had frozen over. How do we respond?

A. We would first respond by asking how, if the Sea of Galilee was frozen, the boat carrying the Apostles was being buffeted by waves and Peter sank into the water as he walked toward Jesus? We would also ask how the Apostles could get a boat a few miles from shore through ice thick enough for a person to walk on it? And then we would wonder if it ever got cold enough in that region of Palestine to freeze the Sea of Galilee. Giuseppe Ricciotti says no in his biography entitled *Life of Christ*:

> "Palestine is a subtropical region and has, practically speaking, only two seasons: the winter, or rainy season from November to April; and the dry, or summer season from May to October. Rains in summer are extremely rare while the average fall of winter rains almost everywhere exceeds 23 inches. Although the temperature varies somewhat with the region, snowfalls are rare and light and occur for the most part in January; frost at night is also rare" (p. 5).

Q. The Gospels say that when Jesus went into the desert, He fasted from food for forty days. But if Jesus was really human, wouldn't He have died of hunger?

A. Matthew says that Jesus fasted for forty days and forty nights, and afterwards He was hungry (cf. 4:2). Luke says that Jesus, "filled with the holy Spirit," was led by the Spirit into the desert, where He spent forty days and was tempted by the Devil. Jesus ate nothing during those days, and when they were over He was hungry (cf. 4:1-2).

As true man, Jesus was subject to the same need for food that all humans are. So how was it possible for Him to go without this basic necessity for that length of time? Perhaps because, as He told the disciples who urged Him to eat something after His conversation with the Samaritan woman, "I have food to eat of which you do not know .... My food is to do the will of the one who sent me and to finish his work" (John 4:32, 34).

Recall, too, that God made it possible for Moses to go without food for forty days on Mount Sinai (Exodus 34:28), so why not Jesus for the same length of time in the desert? Haven't we read of saints who existed for years when their only food was the Holy Eucharist?

All things are possible with God.

Q. Why did Jesus wait four days to come to Lazarus when He heard that His friend was ill?

A. The answer can be found in the Lord's words to the Apostles when they got the message about the condition of Lazarus. "This illness is not to end in death," Jesus said, "but is for the glory of God, that the Son of God may be glorified through it" (John 11:4). When they got to Bethany, the hometown of Lazarus, he had been dead for four days. Jesus met with Lazarus' sisters Martha and Mary and then went to the tomb, where He ordered that the stone be taken away from the opening.

Jesus called Lazarus to come out of the tomb and, when he emerged still bound with the burial cloths, Jesus told the bystanders to set him free (cf. John 11:43-44).

Jesus knew what He was going to do when He delayed coming to Lazarus. He let him die because it would give Him the opportunity to bring His friend back from death, even though Lazarus would die again at a later time. He knew that this miracle would trigger an angry reaction from

His enemies and speed up the conspiracy to have Him put to death. But He was willing to undergo a brutal execution by Crucifixion to demonstrate His power over death and to foreshadow not only His own Resurrection, but also ours as well at the end of the world.

Q. What is the significance of the Transfiguration of Jesus on the mountain?

A. The **Transfiguration** of Jesus (cf. Matthew 17:1-8 and Luke 9:28-36) is a foretaste of Christ's coming in glory at the end of the world. The *Catechism* says (cf. n. 555) that Jesus disclosed His divine glory in order to confirm Peter's statement that He was the Messiah, while at the same time He revealed that before entering into His glory, He would have to die on the Cross in Jerusalem.

According to the same paragraph in the *Catechism*, Moses and Elijah were present because they had announced the suffering of the Messiah, and the bright cloud that overshadowed them indicated the presence of the Holy Spirit. In fact, says the *Catechism*, " 'the whole Trinity appeared: the Father in the voice; the Son in the man; the Spirit in the shining cloud' [St. Thomas Aquinas, *STh* III, 45, 4, *ad* 2]."

A prayer from the Byzantine liturgy explains this well:

> "You were transfigured on the mountain, and your disciples, as much as they were capable of it, beheld your glory, O Christ our God, so that when they should see you crucified they would understand that your Passion was voluntary, and proclaim to the world that you truly are the splendor of the Father."

For more on this, see Tim Gray's book, *Mission of the Messiah* (pp. 91-96), where he lists the striking parallels between the Transfiguration of Jesus and Moses' encounter with God on Mount Sinai.

Q. People used to bow their heads at the mention of Jesus' name, but they don't anymore. How come?

A. A number of religious gestures and signs of reverence have sadly fallen into disuse in recent decades as more and more people have become very careless in their use of God's holy name. One of the great paradoxes of history is that the name of the holiest Person who ever lived on this earth is used to express fear, anger, disgust, and other emotions. Even Catholics who should know better misuse the name of their Lord and Savior.

If, as St. Paul said, "at the name of Jesus/ every knee should bend,/ of those in heaven and on earth and under/ the earth" (Philippians 2:10), those who don't bend their knee ought at least to bow their heads slightly in reverence.

Q. Some people have suggested that there is a distinction between the "Jesus of history" and the "Christ of faith." Is there such a distinction?

A. Only in the minds of those who have a problem believing in the Jesus who is reported in the Gospels as performing miracles and rising from the dead and who attribute these accounts to an anonymous community that came long after Jesus and invented these stories.

Pope Benedict XVI, however, who says in his book *Jesus of Nazareth,* that "I trust in the Gospels" (p. xxi), also says that he "wanted to try to portray the Jesus of the Gospels as the real, 'historical' Jesus in the strict sense of the word. I am convinced, and I hope the reader will be, too, that this figure is much more intelligible than the reconstructions we have been presented with in the last decades. I believe that this Jesus - the Jesus of the Gospels - is a historically plausible and convincing figure" (p. xxii).

The Holy Father goes on to say *(Ibid.)* that "unless there had been something extraordinary in what happened, unless the person and the words of Jesus radically surpassed the hopes and expectations of the time, there is no way to explain why he was crucified or why he made such an impact. As early as twenty or so years after Jesus' death, the great Christ-hymn of the Letter to the Philippians (cf. Phil 2:6-11) offers us a fully developed Christology stating that Jesus was equal to God, but emptied himself, became man, and humbled himself to die on the Cross, and that to him now belongs the worship of all creation, the adoration that God, through the Prophet Isaiah, said was due to him alone (cf. Is 45:23)."

To say that this Christology is "the fruit of anonymous collective formulations, whose authorship we seek to discover," says Benedict, "does not actually explain anything. How could these unknown groups be so creative? How were they so persuasive and how did they manage to prevail? Isn't it more logical, even historically speaking, to assume that the greatness came at the beginning, and that the figure of Jesus really did explode all existing categories and could only be understood in the light of the mystery of God?" (pp. xxii-xxiii).

Q. How do we answer those who say that Jesus is only one way of salvation?
A. By referring them to *Dominus Iesus*, a document issued in 2000 by the Congregation for the Doctrine of the Faith that reaffirmed the indispensable role of Jesus Christ in the salvation of humanity. "It must be *firmly believed*," the document said, "that, in the mystery of Jesus Christ, the incarnate Son of God, who is 'the way, and the truth, and the life' (Jn. 14:6), the full revelation of divine truth is given .... Therefore, the theory of the limited, incomplete, or imperfect character of the revelation of Jesus Christ, which would be complementary to that found in other religions, is contrary to the Church's faith .... It must therefore be *firmly believed* as a truth of the Catholic Faith that the universal salvific will of the one and triune God is offered and accomplished once for all in the mystery of the Incarnation, Death, and Resurrection of the Son of God" (nn. 5, 6, 14).

Chapter 3

Jesus and His Mother

Q. Do Catholics worship Mary and make her equal to Jesus?

A. No, Catholics only worship God, but they do pay high honor and reverence to Mary for the holy life she led and because she was chosen by God to be the mother of His Son. The Fourth Commandment tells us to honor mothers and fathers. Did Jesus keep this commandment by honoring His mother? Of course He did. So in honoring Mary we are just following the example of our Lord. What's wrong with honoring the holiest woman who ever lived? The woman whose "yes" made it possible for us to get to Heaven?

The Bible tells us to call Mary "blessed" (Luke 1:48), so Catholics are just following Scripture when they pay tribute to the Blessed Mother. Does this tribute take away from our worship of Jesus? Not at all. Devotion to Mary always leads us to her Son. Mary's final words in the Gospels, speaking about her Son at the wedding feast in Cana, suggest the course that we are to follow: "Do whatever he tells you" (John 2:5).

Q. How can we call Mary "ever-virgin" when the Gospels say that Jesus had "brothers" and "sisters"?

A. It has been the constant teaching of the Catholic Church for 2,000 years that Mary had no children other than Jesus and that she was a virgin before, during, and after the birth of our Lord, which is why we speak of her as **"ever-virgin."** Search the New Testament from beginning to end and you will not find Mary identified as the mother of anyone but Jesus.

Yes, there are a number of references in the Gospels to the "brothers" and "sisters" of Jesus, but that's because there was no word for cousin or other relatives in Hebrew or Aramaic, languages that Jesus and the disciples spoke, and so these persons were referred to as brothers and sisters. For example, the James and Joseph mentioned as brothers of Jesus in Matthew 13:55 were in fact the sons of another Mary, the wife of Clopas (Matthew 27:56). Since the Gospels tell us that Mary of Clopas was the Blessed Mother's "sister" (John 19:25), that means that she was Jesus' aunt and her children were His cousins.

It was not uncommon in those days, or in our own time either, to call close friends or relatives "brothers" or "sisters," as Jesus did in John 20:17, when He told Mary Magdalene to "go to my brothers and tell them, 'I am going to my Father and your Father, to my God and your God.' " But Magdalene went not to any blood brothers of Jesus, but "to the disciples" (John 20:18). Or as Peter did in Acts 1:16, when he addressed the 120 disciples gathered in the Upper Room as "my brothers."

Furthermore, if our Lord had blood brothers, wouldn't He on the Cross have entrusted His mother to their care rather than to the Apostle John (cf. John 19:26-27)?

Q. But what about Luke's statement (2:7) that Mary gave birth to "her firstborn son"? Or Matthew's statement (1:25) that Joseph "had no relations with her until she bore a son"?

A. That Jesus was Mary's "firstborn" son means only that He was her first child, the child who opened the womb and belonged to God (cf. Exodus 13:2, 34:20). It does not mean that there were other children later on. This first-born son had to be taken to the Temple and consecrated to the Lord by offering a sacrifice of either a pair of turtledoves or two young pigeons (cf. Luke 2:23-24).

As for the statement from Matthew, the problem is that we interpret the word "until" to mean that something happened after that. But in the Bible "until" (or "till") meant only that something had not happened up to that point in time. It did not imply, as it does today, that some action did happen later.

Consider an example from the Old Testament that shows how absurd this interpretation can be if the modern sense is applied to the Bible. In 2 Samuel 6:23, it says that "Saul's daughter Michal was childless to [till] the day of her death." Does this mean that she had children *after* her death?

Q. What of the contention that St. Joseph was a widower with several children prior to marrying the Blessed Virgin Mary? Could these children have been the "brothers" and "sisters" of Jesus?

A. While the *Protoevangelium of James*, an extra-biblical book probably written late in the second century, makes Joseph out to be a widower with children from a previous marriage when he married Mary, there is nothing in the canonical books of the Bible to support this theory. Some who advance this possibility may be trying to account for Joseph's willingness to enter into a celibate marriage, but Pope John Paul shed a different light on Mary and Joseph's consecrated virginity at an audience on August 21, 1996:

> "It may be presumed that at the time of their betrothal there was an understanding between Joseph and Mary about her plan to live as a virgin. Moreover, the Holy Spirit, who had inspired Mary to choose virginity in view of the mystery of the Incarnation and who wanted the latter to come about in a family setting suited to the Child's growth, was quite able to instill in Joseph the ideal of virginity as well."

In his book *To Know Christ Jesus* (pp. 71-72), Frank Sheed also rejected this theory, saying that "such an arrangement, with Joseph merely brought in to keep the neighbors from talking, would hardly be a marriage at all, but rather a mockery of marriage .... We must think of them as truly husband and wife, with a true union of personalities, each bringing completion to the other, with a profound sharing of interests, sharing of lives, enriched by the special graces from God that their virginity called for ....

"Both loved God supremely, and their love of God poured back in a great flood of love of each other, love so great that it made the ordinary outward manifestation unnecessary. There was more love in that virginal family, more married love, than ever a family has known."

Q. Some say that Mary was an unwed mother. How do we answer that?

A. Matthew says that when "Mary was betrothed to Joseph, but before they lived together, she was found with child through the holy Spirit. Joseph her husband, since he was a righteous man, yet unwilling to expose her to shame, decided to divorce her quietly" (1:18-19).

What needs to be understood is that betrothal then did not mean what it means today, i.e., an engagement leading eventually to marriage. According to Jewish tradition, betrothal was the ceremony that united the couple in marriage. The second stage came a year later, if the woman was a virgin, when she moved into the house of her husband.

In his apostolic exhortation *Guardian of the Redeemer,* Pope John Paul II confirmed this tradition:

> "According to Jewish custom, marriage took place in two stages: first, the legal or true marriage was celebrated and, then, only after a certain period of time, the husband brought the wife into his own house. Thus, before he lived with Mary, Joseph was already her 'husband.' Mary, however, preserved her deep desire to give herself exclusively to God" (n. 18).

Even someone unfamiliar with Jewish custom, however, can, by reading Matthew 1:18-19 carefully, discern that Mary and Joseph were married before Jesus was conceived by the power of the Holy Spirit. Matthew calls Joseph Mary's "husband" and says that Joseph had decided to "divorce her quietly" when he discovered that she was with child upon returning from a three-month visit to Elizabeth, her kinswoman and mother of John the Baptist. But how could Joseph divorce Mary unless they were already married?

Q. What does it mean in Luke 2:35, where Simeon says that Mary's heart will be pierced with a sword "so that the thoughts of many hearts may be revealed"?

A. It would be helpful to quote Simeon's entire statement as he took the Christ Child into his arms: "Behold, this child is destined for the fall and rise of many in Israel, and to be a sign that will be contradicted (and you yourself a sword will pierce) so that the thoughts of many hearts may be revealed" (Luke 2:34-35).

This means that Mary will also suffer along with her Son not only on the road to Calvary and at the foot of the Cross, but also when He and His teachings provoked animosity and hatred among His listeners as people chose sides and showed by words and actions the thoughts contained within their hearts. Jesus was able to read those hostile hearts and to know what His enemies were thinking and planning. Simeon was predicting that spiritual downfall would come to those who rejected Jesus, while those who chose to follow Him would rise spiritually in the sight of God.

He was also prophesying that Mary would experience what are now known as her "Seven Sorrows." Those sorrows are the prophecy of Simeon, the flight into Egypt to escape the murderous wrath of King Herod, the three-day separation from Jesus in Jerusalem when He was twelve years old, the meeting with her Son on the road to Calvary, the Crucifixion and Death of our Lord, the placing of His body in Mary's arms after it was taken down from the Cross, and the burial of Jesus in the tomb provided by Joseph of Arimathea.

Q. How do we reconcile the timing of the flight of the Holy Family into Egypt with the Presentation of Jesus in the Temple in Jerusalem?

A. Unlike modern-day historians, the Evangelists were not all that concerned with the precise chronological sequence of events, and one has to look at both Matthew and Luke to piece together the Infancy narrative. According to the Mosaic law, a woman who had delivered a male child was to present herself in the Temple for purification forty days after the birth and also to consecrate a first-born son to the Lord, and then redeem him for five shekels.

Thus, Mary and Joseph traveled to Jerusalem forty days after the birth of Christ and fulfilled both prescriptions of the law. They then returned to Bethlehem and were living in a house when the Magi arrived. So the Presentation took place before the arrival of the trio and the flight into Egypt.

The Magi had been asked by King Herod to let him know the location of the newly born king of the Jews so that he could go and pay Him homage (in reality to kill Him). But they were warned in a dream of Herod's evil intentions and returned home by another route. The same angelic warning was given to Joseph in a dream, and he quickly set out for Egypt with Mary and the Christ Child.

The Holy Family remained in Egypt, where there was a large Jewish colony, until word came of Herod's death, and the refugees returned to their own country, eventually settling in Nazareth. The Gospels do not give us the exact duration of their sojourn in Egypt, but reliable historians, such as Giuseppe Ricciotti (cf. *The Life of Christ*, pp. 257-259), estimate that their stay may have been only a few months.

Q. How do we know that Mary was conceived without Original Sin and was sinless all her life? After all, in her Magnificat she talked about God as "my savior" (Luke 1:47).

A. First of all, we are <u>not</u> talking here about the virginal conception of Jesus in Mary's womb through the power of the Holy Spirit; that is the doctrine of her Divine Maternity. Mary's **Immaculate Conception** means that, from the first instant of her conception in the womb of her mother, she was preserved from all stain of Original Sin. This doctrine is implied in the greeting of the angel Gabriel to the young Jewish maiden (Confraternity Version): "Hail, full of grace, the Lord is with thee" (Luke 1:28).

If Mary was full of grace at the time of the angel's visit, which is known as the **Annunciation**, that means that she was entirely full of God's divine life and therefore free from all sin. Jesus gave her this special privilege because He wanted to be born of a pure and sinless mother. While the Church has always taught this doctrine, it was not until 1854 that Blessed Pope Pius IX infallibly proclaimed it a dogma of the Church. It is also a teaching of the Church (cf. the *Catechism*, n. 493) that by the grace of God Mary remained free of every personal sin during her entire life.

As for her reference to "my savior," the Blessed Mother, as a descendant of Adam, also required a savior and could have contracted Original Sin at the moment her life began, but God preserved her from this plague of the human race and from all its consequences. She was redeemed by the blood of Christ, not through baptism but by anticipation.

The Church has for centuries explained this doctrine with the analogy of a deep hole with the words "Original Sin" on the muddy bottom. All members of the human race, except Mary, fall into this pit and are stained with Original Sin. The only way that they can be rescued or "saved" from the pit is through the sacrament of Baptism.

Mary, on the other hand, was prevented from even falling into the hole, from being stained with Original Sin. Jesus applied His grace to her before she could topple into the pit and be marred with that sin.

Q. But what about the teaching that Mary was taken bodily to Heaven at the end of her life?

A. The **Assumption** of the Blessed Virgin Mary is the corollary to her Immaculate Conception, and the reasoning behind it is that, since Mary was free from Original Sin, and the corruption of the body in the grave is a consequence of that sin, she did not suffer the decay of the grave. It is not unreasonable to say that Jesus would want His mother to share in His bodily glorification since it was her body that sheltered Him for nine months.

Publicly stated belief in this doctrine can be traced back at least to the sixth century, when St. Gregory of Tours wrote that the Lord Jesus came to earth at the end of Mary's life and commanded that her holy body "be taken in a cloud into Paradise, where now, rejoined to the soul, it rejoices with the Lord's chosen ones, and is in the enjoyment of the good of an eternity that will never end."

It wasn't until 1950, however, that Pope Pius XII, after consulting with bishops all over the world, infallibly proclaimed as a divinely revealed dogma "that the Immaculate Mother of God, Mary ever-Virgin, on the completion of her earthly life, was taken up to heavenly glory both in body and soul."

Q. How can Mary, a human being, be called the Mother of God, who is divine?

A. When a mother gives birth, she gives birth to a person, not to a nature. So the Child growing in Mary's womb for nine months was fully human, but was not only human. The Second Person of the Blessed Trinity was also divine, having always possessed a divine nature. He received His human nature from His mother, who supplied all of the genetic matter for His human body. She was not just the mother of His human nature, however, but the mother of Himself. If Mary is the mother of Jesus, and Jesus is God, then Mary is the Mother of God.

When a heretic named Nestorius denied the real union of the divine and human natures in Christ and taught that while Mary could be called the Mother of Christ as man, she could not be called the Mother of God, the Council of Ephesus declared in 431:

> "We confess, then, our Lord Jesus Christ, the only begotten Son of God, perfect God and perfect man, of a rational soul and a body, begotten before all ages from the Father in His Godhead, the same in the last days for us and for our salvation, born of Mary the Virgin according to His humanity, one and the same consubstantial with the Father in Godhead and consubstantial with us in humanity, for a union of two natures took place. Therefore, we confess one Christ, one Son, one Lord. According to this understanding of the unconfused union, we confess the holy Virgin to be the Mother of God because God the Word took flesh and became man and from His very conception united to Himself the temple He took from her."

Q. Why did Jesus call Mary "woman" instead of "Mother" at the wedding in Cana and from the Cross?

A. While this might sound disrespectful to us today, it was a common and rather formal way of speaking at the time of Jesus. But it was also our Lord's way of connecting His mother with the "woman" mentioned in Genesis 3:15, who would be the enemy of Satan and whose offspring would bring about the final victory over Satan, sin, and death.

The Church has always seen Mary as that woman, the "New Eve" whose obedience would, in the words of St. Irenaeus, "untie the knot of Eve's disobedience," and Jesus as her offspring, who would be the "new Adam" by "becoming obedient to death,/ even death on a cross" (Philippians 2:8).

Q. Why does the Church teach that Mary is our mother when Jesus mentioned her only as John's mother?

A. The teaching that Mary is our mother is based on Jesus' words from the Cross: "When Jesus saw his mother and the disciple there whom he loved, he said to his mother, 'Woman, behold your son.' Then he said to the disciple, 'Behold, your mother.' And from that hour the disciple took her into his home" (John 19:26-27).

The Church has always seen the disciple John as representing us at the foot of the Cross, so when Jesus told him that Mary was to be his mother (bear in mind that John's mother was also there at the Cross), He was making clear that Mary was to be the mother of us all. In his encyclical *Mother of the Redeemer*, Pope John Paul II explained it this way:

> "The words uttered by Jesus from the Cross signify that the motherhood of her who bore Christ finds a 'new' continuation in the Church and through the Church, symbolized and represented by John. In this way, she who as the one 'full of grace' was brought into the mystery of Christ in order to be his mother and thus the Holy Mother of God, through the Church remains in that mystery as 'the woman' spoken of by the book of Genesis (3:15) at the beginning and by the Apocalypse (12:1) at the end of the history of salvation.

> "In accordance with the eternal plan of Providence, Mary's divine motherhood is to be poured out upon the Church, as indicated by statements of Tradition, according to which Mary's 'motherhood' of the Church is the reflection and extension of her motherhood of the Son of God" (n. 24).

Q. Shouldn't we pray directly to Jesus instead of to Mary? Doesn't prayer to Mary undermine Jesus' role as the one mediator with God?

A. Of course, we can pray directly to Jesus, and there is no question that Jesus is the one, unique mediator between God and us. But does this mean that Christ doesn't want anyone else sharing in His mediating role, not even His mother, whose intercessory prayer to her Son resulted in the miracle at Cana? Why would Jesus not listen to prayers from the Blessed Virgin Mary, whom He gave to us as our mother from the Cross?

Here on earth we often ask people for prayers, particularly those whom we believe to be holy. Why not ask the holiest woman who ever lived, and whom we know is now with her Son in Heaven, to intercede for us with the One who could not deny any request from His mother? "To Jesus through Mary" has long been a motto for Catholics, and many prayers have been answered through the intercession of the holy Mother of God.

Jesus and His Mother

Chapter 4

Jesus and the Church

Q. Some Scripture scholars contend that Jesus did not come to earth specifically to start a new religion with a code of rules and regulations, but rather to show people a new way to live in the world and to gain the gift of salvation. Is this correct?

A. Only partially. Yes, Jesus indeed came to show people a new way to live in the world so they could gain salvation, but He also established a new covenant (cf. 1 Corinthians 11:25) and a new religion or church (cf. Matthew 16:18) as the vehicle for salvation. In the words of the Second Vatican Council's *Dogmatic Constitution on the Church:*

> "Christ, the one Mediator, established and ceaselessly sustains here on earth his holy Church, the community of faith, hope, and charity, as a visible structure. Through her He communicates truth and grace to all .... This is the unique Church of Christ which in the Creed we avow as one, holy, catholic, and apostolic. After his Resurrection, our Savior handed her over to Peter to be shepherded (Jn. 21:17), commissioning him and the other apostles to propagate and govern her (cf. Mt. 28:18ff.). Her He erected for all ages as 'the pillar and mainstay of the truth' (1 Tim. 3:15). This Church, constituted and organized in the world as a society, subsists in the Catholic Church, which is governed by the successor of Peter and by the bishops in union with that successor" (n. 8).

Since Jesus also gave Peter, and his successors, the power of binding and loosing (cf. Matthew 16:19), i.e., the power to make laws and to set them aside, He must have intended that His Church set forth for the faithful certain rules and regulations. The Church has done precisely that in the Code of Canon Law and in the Precepts of the Church.

Q. How do we know that Jesus started a church?

A. By looking at Matthew's Gospel, chapter 16, verses 15-19. After asking the Apostles who they thought He was, and hearing Simon Peter's response that "you are the Messiah, the Son of the living God," Jesus said to Simon:

> "Blessed are you, Simon son of Jonah. For flesh and blood has not revealed this to you, but my heavenly Father. And so I say to you, you are Peter, and upon this rock I will build my church, and the gates of the netherworld shall not prevail against it. I will give you the keys to the kingdom of heaven. Whatever you bind on earth shall be bound in heaven; and whatever you loose on earth shall be loosed in heaven."

Note that Jesus not only chose Peter to be the first head of His Church, but He also said that the powers of evil would never prevail against His Church and that Peter would have the authority to make laws for the Church on earth that would have the approval of Jesus in Heaven. Furthermore, our Lord said that His Church would last forever and that He would remain with her "always, until the end of the age" (Matthew 28:20).

In chapter 18 of Matthew, verse 17, Jesus mentioned His Church again, this time stressing the role of the Church in disciplining a member who has sinned and who has resisted correction by other members of the Church. Apparently, members of Christ's Church were expected to abide by certain rules and regulations.

Q. How do we answer those who say that Jesus was not speaking to Peter, but to us, in Matthew 16, and that He gave the keys to the kingdom to us?

A. Here is what the *Catechism of the Catholic Church* says:

> "Jesus entrusted a specific authority to Peter: 'I will give you the keys of the kingdom of heaven, and

whatever you bind on earth shall be bound in heaven, and whatever you loose on earth shall be loosed in heaven' [Mt 16:19]. The 'power of the keys' designates authority to govern the house of God, which is the Church. Jesus, the Good Shepherd, confirmed this mandate after his Resurrection: 'Feed my sheep' [Jn 21:15-17; cf. 10:11]. The power to 'bind and loose' connotes the authority to absolve sins, to pronounce doctrinal judgments, and to make disciplinary decisions in the Church. Jesus entrusted this authority to the Church through the ministry of the apostles [cf. Mt 18:18] and in particular through the ministry of Peter, the only one to whom he specifically entrusted the keys of the kingdom" (n. 553).

As for whether Jesus was really speaking to "us" and giving "us" the keys to the kingdom, one has only to read the passage from Matthew carefully to notice that Jesus *seven times* used the word "you" in reference to Peter.

Q. What about those who say that Peter was never in Rome? Is there any biblical proof that he was?

A. The closest thing to biblical proof that Peter was indeed in Rome can be found in the Apostle's first letter to those in the infant Church, where he says: "The chosen one at Babylon sends you greeting, as does Mark, my son" (1 Peter 5:13). Babylon was a code word used by the early Christians when referring to Rome. The word is used in the same way six times in the Book of Revelation (cf. chapters 14, 16, 17, 18).

Apart from the Bible, there are plenty of references to Peter's being in Rome in the writings of the early Church. For example, Dionysius of Corinth, writing to Pope Soter around the year 170, said: "You have also, by your very admonition, brought together the planting that was made by Peter and Paul at Rome." And St. Irenaeus, also writing in the second century, said that "Matthew also issued among the Hebrews a written Gospel in their own language, while Peter and Paul were evangelizing in Rome and laying the foundation of the Church."

Furthermore, Pope Paul VI announced in 1968 that the skeletal remains of St. Peter had been found and satisfactorily identified deep under the high altar of St. Peter's Basilica in Rome. For an account of this archaeological discovery, see the book *The Bones of St. Peter* by John Evangelist Walsh.

Q. How can we find today the Church that Jesus started 2,000 years ago?

A. By looking for a church that is led by a successor of Peter and that possesses certain characteristics or signs. The Church has traditionally identified four signs or marks that point to the Church founded by our Lord - she must be one, holy, catholic, and apostolic.

On the matter of leadership, there is clear historical evidence listing the more than 260 men who have sat in the Chair of Peter since the Prince of the Apostles suffered martyrdom in the first century. And there is only one person in the world today who even claims to be the successor of St. Peter and, as this is written, that is Pope Benedict XVI.

Following the example of his well-traveled predecessors, Pope Paul VI and Pope John Paul II, Benedict reiterated his special status in a homily at Nationals Park in Washington, D.C., on April 17, 2008, when he said that, "in the exercise of my ministry as the successor of Peter, I have come to America to confirm you, my brothers and sisters, in the faith of the Apostles (cf. Lk. 22:32). I have come to proclaim anew, as Peter proclaimed on the day of Pentecost, that Jesus Christ is Lord and Messiah, risen from the dead, seated in glory at the right hand of the Father and established as judge of the living and the dead (cf. Acts 2:14ff.)."

Interestingly, even secular leaders recognize this special role of the Holy Father. For example, at a welcoming ceremony on the White House lawn on April 16, 2008, President George W. Bush noted that "this is your first trip to the United States since you ascended to the chair of St. Peter."

Q. Can you explain what is meant by the four marks of the Church: one, holy, catholic, and apostolic?

A. The Church is **one** because Jesus said that His Church would have unity ("There will be one flock, one shepherd" - John 10:16). It is only common sense that Christ would want the members of His Church to be one in what they believe and in how they worship, and that they should be united under one spiritual leader, the Pope. How could Jesus, who is the Truth, say that it doesn't matter what one believes - that there is one God, or three; that Jesus is God, or He is not God; that Hell exists, or it does not exist; that divorce and abortion are wrong, or they are not wrong?

So in the Catholic Church we find unity of belief (cf. the Nicene Creed, Pope Paul VI's *Credo of the People of God*, and the *Catechism of the Catholic Church*); we find unity in worship (no matter where you travel in the world, the same Mass will be celebrated, albeit in a different language, and the same Sacraments will be administered); and we find most Catholics united under the leadership of the Holy Father in Rome and those bishops who are in communion with him.

Because her Founder, the Son of God, is holy, the Church is **holy** - in her purpose (to get us to Heaven); in her Sacraments (those abundant channels of God's grace), especially the Holy Eucharist; in her saints and martyrs; and in her miracles at places like Guadalupe, Fatima, and Lourdes. All Catholics are sinners, some worse than others, but that does not disprove the mark of holiness since the Church is still the Body of Christ on earth and is meant to be a hospital for sinners, not a museum for saints.

The Church is **catholic**, or universal, because she has existed since the time of Christ and can be found everywhere in the world today. Jesus promised to be with His Church until the end of time, so she will last forever, and He told the Apostles, and their successors, to "go into the whole world and proclaim the gospel to every creature. Whoever believes and is baptized will be saved; whoever does not believe will be condemned" (Mark 16:15-16).

Any Church that has not existed since the time of Christ, and is not proclaiming His teachings everywhere today, cannot be His Church.

The Church is **apostolic** in that her origin stems from Peter and the Apostles and that her teachings today are identical with those of the Apostles. No one can reasonably dispute the historical succession of the papacy, from Peter to Benedict XVI (as this is written), and no one can accuse the Catholic Church today of teaching anything except what was taught by Christ Himself and those whom He appointed to direct His Church.

Evidence of this can be found in the Apostles' Creed from the first century, the Nicene Creed from the fourth century, and Pope Paul's *Credo* from the twentieth century. A careful perusal of the *Catechism of the Catholic Church*, which was promulgated in 1992, will also show the continuity and constancy of Catholic teachings over two millennia.

Jesus is still with the Catholic Church today and that Church continues to be what St. Paul called "the pillar and foundation of truth" (1 Timothy 3:15). She could not be otherwise since Jesus promised that He would not leave us orphans, but would ask the Father to "give you another Advocate to be with you always, the Spirit of truth" (John 14:16-17).

Q. But isn't it arrogant for the Catholic Church to claim to be the one Church founded by Jesus Christ?

A. It would be arrogant to make this claim only if the claim were false. But if the claim is true, and we have seen from the previous questions that it is true, then the Catholic Church has an obligation (cf. Matthew 28:19 and Mark 16:15) to make this truth known far and wide since it bears on the eternal salvation of all. One of the strongest assertions of this claim was made by Blessed Pope John XXIII in his 1959 encyclical *To the Chair of Peter.*

The Holy Father first rejected the notion that one religion is as good as another because, he said, that would mean there is no distinction between truth and falsehood. He said that this "absurd proposition" that it doesn't matter what religion a person belongs to "is directed to the destruction of all religions, but particularly the Catholic Faith, which cannot be placed on a level with other religions without serious injustice, <u>since it alone is true</u>" (n. 17).

Other statements of this claim can be found in the Vatican II documents on the Church *(Lumen Gentium)* and ecumenism *(Unitatis Redintegratio)*, Pope John Paul II's encyclicals *Redemptoris Missio* and *Ut Unum Sint*, the previously mentioned *Dominus Iesus*, and the Vatican document *Responses to Some Questions Regarding Certain Aspects of the Doctrine on the Church*, which was issued in 2007 by the Congregation for the Doctrine of the Faith.

In the latter document, which caused quite an uproar, the Congregation reaffirmed that the Church founded by Christ " 'subsists in the Catholic Church, governed by the successor of Peter and the bishops in communion with him.' " It explained that *subsists* was used instead of *is* to show "the full identity of the Church of Christ with the Catholic Church," while at the same time indicating that there are " 'numerous elements of sanctification and of truth' " in the separated Christian communities that can lead them to the Catholic Church. These elements include such things as the written word of God and persons who live lives of grace, faith, hope, and charity.

It is possible, the document said, "to affirm correctly that the Church of Christ is present and operative in the churches and ecclesial communities not yet fully in communion with the Catholic Church, on account of the elements of sanctification and truth that are present in them. Nevertheless, the word *subsists* can be attributed to the Catholic Church alone precisely because it refers to the mark of unity that we possess in the symbols of the faith (I believe ... in the 'one' Church); and this 'one' Church subsists in the Catholic Church."

Those making this claim, of course, must do so humbly and charitably.

Q. What are the names of the twelve Apostles, and do we know what happened to them?

A. Here are their names and the best information we have on what happened to them after the Ascension of Jesus and the coming of the Holy Spirit on Pentecost:

Simon Peter - A fisherman who was introduced to Jesus by his brother Andrew, Peter is the author of two letters in the New Testament. He was not without faults, as when he three times denied that he knew Jesus, but the Lord still chose him to be the first Pope and leader of His Church. After the Resurrection, Jesus three times asked Peter if he loved Him, and three times Peter replied, "Yes, Lord, you know that I love you." And Jesus told him to "feed my lambs ... feed my sheep" (John 21:15-17).

Peter's role as chief shepherd of Jesus' Church is clear in the Acts of the Apostles, where Peter presides over the selection of Matthias to replace Judas (1:15-26), delivers the first sermon on Pentecost and converts 3,000 people (2:14-41), and helps bring the Gospel to the Gentiles by baptizing the Roman official Cornelius (10:44-49) and urging the Council of Jerusalem in A.D. 49 not to require converts to Catholicism to become Jews first (15:1-12).

After being imprisoned in Jerusalem, and being released through the intervention of an angel (Acts 12:6-17), Peter continued to preach there and then traveled to the cities of Antioch, Corinth, and eventually Rome, where he died around the year 65. Tradition has it that he asked to be crucified upside down because his denials of Christ many years before had made him unworthy to die in the same manner as the Master.

Andrew - Also a fisherman and a follower of John the Baptist before being called by Christ, Andrew appears only twice in the Gospels: in John 6:8-9, where he tells Jesus of a boy with five loaves of bread and two fish, which Jesus then multiplied to feed more than 5,000, and in John 12:21-22, where he acts as an intermediary for two Greeks who wanted to meet Jesus.

Church historians record that Andrew preached the Gospel in several parts of what is now Turkey, as well as in parts of Greece. During his missions, he overcame demons, saved the lives of forty shipwrecked people, brought the dead back to life, and was scourged before being crucified on an X-shaped cross in Achaea (now Greece) around the year 60. He was reportedly tied and not nailed to the cross and continued preaching for two days while hanging from the cross. A light from heaven shone around his body, and those who tried to ridicule him were paralyzed. He is the patron saint of Scotland.

James (Son of Zebedee) - Also known as "James the Greater," he was a fisherman and brother of John who belonged to the inner circle of those closest to Jesus. He was with Jesus at the Transfiguration on the Mountain and witnessed His Agony in the Garden of Gethsemane. The first Apostle to die for Christ, James was beheaded by King Herod Agrippa in Jerusalem in A.D. 42. According to tradition, he preached in Spain before his death and, under the name "Santiago," is the patron saint of Spain.

John - Another son of Zebedee and a fisherman, John is known as "the one whom Jesus loved" or the "beloved disciple." He was very close to Jesus, accompanying Him on the Mountain of Transfiguration, leaning his head on the chest of the Lord at the Last Supper, being the only Apostle present at Calvary on Good Friday, and being the one to whom Jesus entrusted the care of His mother. He is the author of the fourth Gospel, three New Testament letters, and the Book of Revelation. According to tradition, John was exiled for a time to the island of Patmos in the Aegean Sea, but spent much of his life in Ephesus, where he reportedly died of old age around the year 100. There is a tradition that an effort was made to kill a younger John by immersing him in boiling oil, but God prevented him from being burned to death.

James (Son of Alphaeus) - Also known as "James the Lesser" either because he was shorter or younger than James the Greater, he was the bishop of Jerusalem and the "brother" or "cousin" of the Lord, and was reportedly stoned to death in Jerusalem in A.D. 62.

Philip - From the same city as Peter and Andrew, he was a follower of John the Baptist and switched his allegiance to Jesus after John called Christ the "Lamb of God." He was involved in the miracle of the loaves and fishes when Jesus asked him where they could buy bread for the crowd and Philip replied that two hundred days' wages wouldn't be enough to feed them all (cf. John 6:5-7). He also joined with Andrew in bringing to Jesus two Greeks who wanted to meet the Lord, and later asked Christ to show them the Father. Jesus replied that whoever had seen Him had seen the Father (cf. John 14:9). Little is known of his later life, although there are traditions that he preached in Asia Minor and died a martyr by being crucified upside down during the reign of the Emperor Domitian (81-96). He had two daughters who were much admired and revered in the early Church.

Bartholomew - Seldom mentioned apart from the lists of the twelve Apostles, he is sometimes known as Nathanael. According to John's Gospel, Bartholomew/Nathanael was recruited by Philip, who told him that they had discovered the Messiah, Jesus from Nazareth. To which Nathanael asked: "Can anything good come from Nazareth?" Philip said, "Come and see." As they were approaching Jesus, the Lord said, "Here is a true Israelite." Nathanael said, "How do you know me?" Jesus replied, "Before Philip called you, I saw you under the fig tree." Nathanael answered, "Rabbi, you are the Son of God; you are the King of Israel" (John 1:45-49). Bartholomew reportedly preached in Armenia and India, Persia and Egypt. Local Armenian officials condemned him to death, slicing the skin off his body and then beheading him.

Thomas - Known as "Doubting Thomas" for the one time when he doubted that Jesus had risen from the dead, he is also known for two other incidents mentioned in John's Gospel. In one case, when the other Apostles were reluctant to go to Jerusalem because they were afraid Jesus would be stoned to death, Thomas said, "Let us also go to die with him" (11:16). At another time, when Jesus told the Apostles that He was going to Heaven to prepare a place for them, Thomas asked how they could know the way? Jesus answered, "I am the way and the truth and the life. No one comes to the Father except through me" (14:6). Thomas is the first person in the Gospels to call Jesus "my Lord and my God" (John 20:28). Little is known of what happened to Thomas later, although it seems likely that he brought Christianity to India around A.D. 52, founded seven churches there, and was martyred in A.D. 72 in Mylapore, Madras, where his tomb is venerated today.

Matthew - Also known as Levi, he was a tax collector who immediately got up from his customs post when Jesus passed by one day and said, "Follow me" (Mark 2:14). He held a dinner for Jesus, which led to criticism of the Lord for eating with tax collectors and sinners. Jesus responded to the criticism by saying, "Those who are well do not need a physician, but the sick do" (Mark 2:17). Matthew is the author of the first Gospel, which concentrates on proving that Jesus is the Messiah by quoting extensively from the Old Testament. It is believed that Matthew preached in Jerusalem, Ethiopia, and Persia (modern-day Iran) and that he was martyred either in Ethiopia or Persia.

Thaddeus - Also known as Jude or Jude Thaddeus or as Judas (not Iscariot), he is the author of the brief New Testament letter bearing his name. He is thought to have been martyred in Persia and is one of the most popular saints in the Church today as the patron of lost causes, but no one knows why this is so.

Simon the Canaanite - Also known as Simon the Zealot because he may have belonged to a group that wanted to overthrow the Roman occupiers of Palestine, he is barely mentioned in the Gospels. According to tradition, he preached in Egypt and in Persia, where he was martyred along with St. Jude.

Judas Iscariot - Always identified as the traitor, Judas is the one who betrayed Jesus to His enemies for 30 pieces of silver. A year before the betrayal, Jesus said that Judas was possessed by a devil (John 6:70), and John calls Judas a thief because he stole money from the Apostles (cf. John 12:6). When Jesus predicted at the Last Supper that one of the Twelve would betray Him, eleven of them said, "Surely it is not I, Lord?" (Matthew 26:22). But Judas said, "Surely it is not I, Rabbi?" (Matthew 26:25). He recognized Jesus only as a teacher, not as the Lord. After Judas saw what was going to happen to Jesus, he tried to give the money back, but it was refused. So he went out and hanged himself from a tree. Is Judas in Hell? Only God knows the answer to that. Perhaps he had the presence of mind to beg for forgiveness just before he died, but we won't know the answer to that until the next life.

Matthias - Chosen to take the place of Judas after the Ascension, Matthias is mentioned only in the Acts of the Apostles. His qualifications to become an Apostle were that he had been with Jesus from the beginning of the Lord's public life, that is, from the time of His Baptism in the River Jordan, and had been a witness to the Resurrection. Matthias preached in Jerusalem and elsewhere and was reportedly stoned to death and then beheaded in Jerusalem.

In his book, *Jesus of Nazareth*, Pope Benedict says that "we may presume that all of the Twelve were believing and observant Jews who awaited the salvation of Israel. But in terms of their actual opinions, of their thinking about the way Israel was to be saved, they were an extremely varied group." He says that "precisely in this wide range of backgrounds, temperaments, and approaches, the Twelve personify the Church of all ages and its difficult task of purifying and unifying these men in the zeal of Jesus Christ" (pp. 178-179).

Q. There seems to be a disagreement among Bible scholars as to whether John is the author of the fourth Gospel. What information do we have?

A. In his book entitled *St. John's Gospel,* Bible scholar Steven K. Ray makes a persuasive case for John's authorship of the fourth Gospel. Among other things, Ray says:

> "The Gospel itself is divinely inspired; the title of the Gospel is not. But that does not leave us without any information about authorship. Internal evidence shows that the author is clearly a Palestinian Jew, fully acquainted with life in Israel before the destruction of Jerusalem. He writes as an eyewitness, with amazing detail, a point that even some Jewish historians have admitted. The writer obviously had an intimate place among Jesus' followers.
>
> "That said, the internal evidence provides only a little

more information. We find references to the disciple 'whom Jesus loved' (Jn 13:23) and the nondescript mention of 'the disciple.' It can be assumed from these references and their context that they refer to the Apostle John, an obvious eyewitness, who in his modesty declines to use his own name and only infrequently quotes his own words (only in Jn 13:25; 21:7; 21:20). But it is the unanimous consent of apostolic tradition that provides certainty as to John's authorship. It is Catholic history and tradition that provide such assurance" (p. 29).

As for external evidence of John's authorship of the fourth Gospel, Ray cites the words of St. Irenaeus, the bishop of Lyons, who wrote in *Against Heresies* (circa 200) that "John, the disciple of the Lord, who also had leaned upon His breast, did himself publish a Gospel during his residence at Ephesus in Asia." He also cites (p. 30) Eusebius (ca. 260-ca. 340), who, after referring to earlier sources, made these comments in his *History of the Church:*

"When Mark and Luke had already published their Gospels, they [the sources] say that John, who had employed all his time in proclaiming the Gospel orally, finally proceeded to write for the following reason. The three Gospels already mentioned having come into the hands of all and into his own, too, they say that he accepted them and bore witness to their truthfulness; but that there was lacking in them an account of the deeds done by Christ at the beginning of his ministry .... They say, therefore, that the Apostle John, being asked to do it for this reason, gave in his Gospel an account of the period which had been omitted by the earlier evangelists, and of the deeds done by the Savior during that period; that is, of those which were done before the imprisonment of the Baptist."

Based on this information, Mr. Ray says, "We can conclude, then, that the Fourth Gospel was written by the Apostle John, about the year 100, from the ancient city of Ephesus" (p. 31).

Q. Why is John the disciple Jesus loved? Didn't He love the other disciples, too, even Judas Iscariot?

A. Jesus certainly did love all of the disciples, including Judas, but He apparently had a special affection for John, perhaps because he was reportedly the youngest member of the Twelve. Our Lord also seemed to favor Peter and James, too, over the other Apostles since He included only them, and John, in such important moments in His life as the Transfiguration and the Agony in the Garden.

Because Jesus was just like us in all things but sin, He liked some people more than others. But He loved everyone, even those who sold Him out and executed Him. Recall that even as Judas was about to betray Him with a kiss in the Garden of Gethsemane, Jesus reached out once more to him, calling him "friend" (Matthew 26:50), but there was no turning back for Judas.

Jesus at the Last Supper

Chapter 5

Jesus and the Sacraments

Q. What are the Sacraments?

A. According to the *Catechism of the Catholic Church*, the Sacraments are "efficacious signs of grace, instituted by Christ and entrusted to the Church, by which divine life is dispensed to us" (n. 1131). They are also visible signs of an invisible reality, namely, God's love. They are actions through which Christ gives His Spirit to us and makes us a holy people. They are special encounters in which we meet God and God meets us.

But whatever definition we use, it is important to understand that the Sacraments, in the words of the U.S. Bishops' document *Basic Teachings for Catholic Religious Education,* "are always to be thought of as actions of Christ himself, from whom they get their power. Thus, it is Christ who baptizes, Christ who offers himself in the Sacrifice of the Mass through the ministry of the priests, and Christ who forgives sins in the Sacrament of Penance" (n. 10).

Q. Can it be demonstrated that Jesus gave us seven Sacraments?

A. Yes, it can. Jesus is specifically mentioned in connection with five Sacraments (Baptism, Holy Eucharist, Penance, Holy Orders, and Matrimony), and the other two are mentioned in the New Testament in connection with Peter and John (Confirmation) and James (Anointing of the Sick). Here are the biblical sources for all seven:

Baptism - In his final appearance to the Apostles, Jesus told them: "Go, therefore, and make disciples of all nations, baptizing them in the name of the Father, and of the Son, and of the holy Spirit" (Matthew 28:19).

Confirmation - While visiting Samaria, Peter and John found that the Christians there "had only been baptized in the name of the Lord Jesus. Then they laid hands on them and they received the holy Spirit" (Acts 8:16-17).

Holy Eucharist - After taking bread and wine in His hands at the Last Supper, Jesus said: "This is my body .... This cup is the new covenant in my blood .... Do this in memory of me" (Matthew 26:28, Luke 22:19-20, cf. 1 Corinthians 11:23-25).

Penance/Reconciliation - In His appearance to the Apostles on the first Easter Sunday night, Jesus "breathed on them and said to them, 'Receive the holy Spirit. Whose sins you forgive are forgiven them, and whose sins you retain are retained'" (John 20:22-23).

Anointing of the Sick - In his letter, James said: "Is anyone among you sick? He should summon the presbyters of the church, and they should pray over him and anoint [him] with oil in the name of the Lord, and the prayer of faith will save the sick person, and the Lord will raise him up. If he has committed any sins, he will be forgiven" (James 5:14-15).

Holy Orders - At the Last Supper, Jesus, after offering up bread and wine, told the Apostles, his first priests, to "do this in memory of me" (Luke 22:19). Later, St. Luke tells us, when Paul and Barnabas were traveling from place to place, "they appointed presbyters [priests] for them in each church and, with prayer and fasting, commended them to the Lord in whom they had put their faith" (Acts 14:23).

Matrimony - Responding to a question about marriage and divorce, Jesus said to the Pharisees: "Have you not read that from the beginning the Creator 'made them male and female' and said, 'For this reason a man shall leave his father and mother and be joined to his wife, and the two shall become one flesh'? So they are no longer two, but one flesh. Therefore, what God has joined together, no human being must separate" (Matthew 19:4-6).

Q. Why do Catholics tell their sins to a priest? Why not confess directly to God?

A. We can confess our sins directly to God, and we should say an Act of Contrition every night, expressing sorrow for any sins committed that day. But Jesus wanted us to obtain forgiveness through a priest. On Easter Sunday night, He told the Apostles, His first priests: "Receive the holy Spirit. Whose sins you forgive are forgiven them, and whose sins you retain are retained" (John 20:22-23). Notice Jesus said, "Whose sins you forgive," not whose sins I forgive, although He is ultimately the one extending forgiveness. Furthermore, if the priest is to "retain" or not forgive someone's sins, he must first be told the sins in order to decide whether to grant God's forgiveness or not.

There are also advantages to telling one's sins to a priest in Confession. It teaches us humility, imparts grace to us, gives us the assurance that our sins have been forgiven when the priest pronounces the words of absolution, and lets the priest give us advice on how to avoid sins in the future.

In his statement on *Reconciliation and Penance*, Pope John Paul II urged Catholics to confess their sins often to a priest, saying that "it would therefore be foolish, as well as presumptuous, to wish arbitrarily to disregard the means of grace and salvation which the Lord has provided and ... to claim to receive forgiveness while doing without the sacrament which was instituted by Christ precisely for forgiveness" (n. 31).

Q. How do we respond to those who say that Jesus did not multiply the loaves and fishes, but rather persuaded the people to share their own food with each other?

A. We can suggest that they read all six Gospel accounts of the multiplication of bread and fish and show us one place where Jesus talked about "sharing food." They won't find a single one. To say that this was not a miracle is to say that Matthew, Mark, Luke, and John either were stupid and didn't know what Jesus was really doing, or they lied about it. The truth, of course, is that it was a miracle.

Furthermore, if we read the account of this miracle in chapter 6 of John's Gospel, for example, we will see how foolish it is to say that it never happened. For one thing, the crowd wanted to make Jesus a king after He had fed them. Why would they want to do that if all He had done was inspire them to share their food with others? And why the following day, on the other side of the lake, did the same people want Jesus to perform the same miracle again, if there were no miracle in the first place?

Recall the words of Jesus: "I am the living bread that came down from heaven; whoever eats this bread will live forever; and the bread that I will give is my flesh for the life of the world" (John 6:51). So beware of those who would undermine the divinity of Jesus by saying that His miracles were not really miracles at all.

Q. How do we know that Jesus is really present in the Holy Eucharist?

A. By believing exactly what He said to us about this wonderful sacrament. At the Last Supper, when Jesus said the first Mass, He took bread and said, "This is my body." He did not say, "This represents my body." He took wine and said, "This is my blood." He did not say, "This is a symbol of my blood." It is ironic that those who take the words of Christ so literally elsewhere in the Gospels disregard the literalness of these words.

Further evidence of this truth that Jesus intended to convey can be found in chapter 6 of John's Gospel, where He said, "Unless you eat the flesh of the Son of Man and drink his blood, you do not have life within you. Whoever eats my flesh and drinks my blood has eternal life, and I will raise him on the last day. For my flesh is true food, and my blood is true drink" (6:53-55).

Some of those listening to Jesus thought He was crazy and walked away, but Jesus didn't say, "Wait a minute, friends, that's not what I meant. Come on back." No, He let them walk away because that's exactly what He meant. So Catholic belief in the Real Presence of Jesus in the Eucharist is based on the words of Christ Himself.

In their document on *The Real Presence of Jesus Christ in the Sacrament of the Eucharist: Basic Questions and Answers,* the U.S. Bishops responded to the question, "Are the consecrated bread and wine 'merely symbols'?" in this way:

"The transformed bread and wine that are the Body and Blood of Christ are not merely symbols because they truly are the Body and Blood of Christ. As St. John Damascene wrote: 'The bread and wine are not a foreshadowing of the Body and Blood of Christ - by no means! - but the actual deified Body of the Lord because the Lord himself said: 'This is my body'; not 'a foreshadowing of my body' but 'my body,' and not 'a foreshadowing of my blood' but 'my blood' " *(The Orthodox Faith,* IV [PG 94, 1148-49]).

Q. How do we answer the charge of "cannibalism" when we eat the Body and Blood of Christ?

A. This thought no doubt prompted the exodus of some of those who heard Jesus' discourse on the Eucharist as reported in John 6. But here are some thoughts on how the charge can be answered.

Cannibalism can be defined as the eating of a dead human body by other humans. If Jesus' followers had taken His body down from the Cross and eaten it, *that* would have been cannibalism. There are two orders here, the *natural order* and the *supernatural order.* Eating His body in the natural order would mean eating His corpse and, once that was done, there would be no body left. Eating His body and blood in the supernatural order, however, is not cannibalism because Christ is not present in the Eucharist in a natural way, but in a supernatural way. The Eucharist we receive in the natural order has the natural qualities of bread and wine, not of a human body, although it has been changed, supernaturally, by Christ into His body and blood, as He did at the Last Supper.

This corresponds with the supernatural relationship we have with Him through Christian Baptism, in which we receive a supernatural principle of life in union with Christ, with Him living in us and we in Him. All of the sacraments were instituted by Christ for this purpose, each in its own particular way, to bring about our perfect union with Him, and in this consists our sanctification.

Q. What is the precise definition of the word "transubstantiation?"

A. Transubstantiation is a theological term that describes the unique change of the entire substance of the bread into the Body of Christ and the entire substance of the wine into the Blood of Christ, even though the appearances, or accidents, of the bread and wine remain. By accidents we mean the color, weight, taste, and shape of the elements that have become the Body and Blood of Christ. This change in substance takes place when the priest at Mass says the words of our Lord: "This is my body .... This is the cup of my blood." The Real Presence of Christ endures as long as the appearances of bread and wine remain (cf. *Catechism of the Catholic Church*, n. 1377).

In the *Credo of the People of God*, Pope Paul VI explained how we are to understand this change:

> "Christ cannot be thus present in this sacrament except by the change into his body of the reality itself of the bread and the change into his blood of the reality itself of the wine,

leaving unchanged only the properties of the bread and wine which our senses perceive. This mysterious change is very appropriately called by the Church *transubstantiation.*

"Every theological explanation which seeks some understanding of this mystery must, in order to be in accord with Catholic faith, maintain that in the reality itself, independent of our mind, the bread and wine have ceased to exist after the Consecration, so that it is the adorable Body and Blood of the Lord Jesus that from then on are really before us under the sacramental species of bread and wine, as the Lord willed it, in order to give himself to us as food and to associate us with the unity of his Mystical Body."

Q. How is it possible for bread and wine to become the Body and Blood of Christ?

A. Each of us has grown since we were children and today we have more flesh and blood than we had back then. Our body changed the food we ate into flesh and blood. If the human body can do that, God can do it also.

Q. How is it possible for the whole Body and Blood of Christ to be present in Catholic churches all over the world, in every Host and in every part of each Host?

A. For God, nothing is impossible. However, something similar happens in everyday life. When we look into a large mirror, we see our image reflected only once. But when the mirror is broken into a hundred pieces, we can see the image of ourself in each piece. So, too, Christ can be present in many places at the same time.

Q. How is Jesus present in the Mass?

A. Jesus is present in the Mass in a variety of ways, but most especially in the Holy Eucharist. Here is what Vatican II said in the *Constitution on the Sacred Liturgy* (n. 7):

"Christ is always present in His Church, especially in her liturgical celebrations. He is present in the sacrifice of the Mass, not only in the person of His minister, 'the same one now offering, through the ministry of priests, who formerly offered Himself on the Cross,' but especially under the Eucharistic species. By His power He is present in the sacraments, so that when a man baptizes it is really Christ Himself who baptizes. He is present in His word, since it is He Himself who speaks when the holy Scriptures are read in the church. He is present, finally, when the Church prays and sings, for He promised: 'Where two or three are gathered together for my sake, there am I in the midst of them' (Mt. 18:20)."

Q. Why didn't Jesus ordain women as priests?

A. Jesus certainly had plenty of worthy women who supported Him during His ministry, including His own mother, whom He could have ordained to the priesthood, but He chose to ordain only men. This was not a put down of women, since Jesus demonstrated high regard for the women of His time, including the Samaritan woman at the well (John 4:4-42) and Mary Magdalene, who had the privilege of being the first person to see Jesus after His Resurrection (John 20:11-18).

Jesus never made any definitive statement about a male-only priesthood, but we can surmise that since He is our Eternal High Priest who chose to come to earth as a man, and since priests are supposed to be icons or representations of Christ, who stand in the person of Christ at the altar, He thought it fitting that only men should be priests. If we were going to choose someone to stand in the person of the Blessed Virgin, we wouldn't choose a man.

Furthermore, since Christ is often referred to as the Bridegroom and the Church as His bride, that symbolism would be lost with women priests since the heavenly Bridegroom would be represented by a bride and you would have the confusing situation of two brides instead of a bride and groom.

So the Church is just following the example of her Founder in ordaining only men. As Pope John Paul II stated infallibly in his apostolic letter on this subject *(Ordinatio Sacerdotalis)*:

> "Wherefore, in order that all doubt may be removed regarding a matter which pertains to the Church's divine constitution itself, in virtue of my ministry of confirming the brethren (cf. Lk. 22:32) I declare that the Church has no authority whatsoever to confer priestly ordination on women and that this judgment is to be definitively held by all the Church's faithful" (n. 4).

Lastly, the Church cannot ordain everybody. Every sacrament must have the right "matter." You can't baptize with Pepsi, you can't change water into the Blood of Christ. Water isn't inferior to wine, anymore than women are inferior to men. Man and woman, like water and wine, are of equal dignity, but because Christ chose only men to be priests, only baptized males are the proper matter for Holy Orders, just as only bread and wine are the proper matter for the Holy Eucharist.

Moses receiving the Ten Commandments

Chapter 6

Jesus' Moral Code

Q. What do we say to those who claim that the Commandments are "Old Testament morality" and that Jesus never talked about them?

A. We suggest that they read about Jesus' encounter with the rich young man in chapter 19 of Matthew (or chapter 10 of Mark or chapter 18 of Luke). The man asked Christ what he must do to possess everlasting life, and Jesus told him to keep the commandments. The man then asked, "Which ones?" and Christ replied: " 'You shall not kill; you shall not commit adultery; you shall not steal; you shall not bear false witness; honor your father and your mother'; and 'you shall love your neighbor as yourself' " (Matthew 19:17-19).

The Ten Commandments, of course, are only the minimum required to be a follower of Christ. It is not enough, Jesus said in the Sermon on the Mount, to say that you have never murdered anyone, for "I say to you, whoever is angry with his brother will be liable to judgment" (Matthew 5:22). It is not enough, Jesus said, to say that you have never committed adultery, for "I say to you, everyone who looks at a woman with lust has already committed adultery with her in his heart" (Matthew 5:28).

Are the Ten Commandments still binding today? Yes, says the *Catechism of the Catholic Church*:

> "Since they express man's fundamental duties towards God and towards his neighbor, the Ten Commandments reveal, in their primordial content, *grave* obligations. They are fundamentally immutable, and they oblige always and everywhere. No one can dispense from them. The Ten Commandments are engraved by God on the human heart" (n. 2072).

Q. What commandments was Jesus talking about in John 15:10, when He said, "If you keep my commandments, you will remain in my love, just as I have kept my Father's commandments and remain in his love"?

A. Our Lord could have been referring either to the Ten Commandments or to the two great commandments, which He spelled out for a Pharisee who asked Him which commandment in the law was the greatest of them all. Jesus replied:

> "You shall love the Lord, your God, with all your heart, with all your soul, and with all your mind. This is the greatest and the first commandment. The second is like it: You shall love your neighbor as yourself. The whole law and the prophets depend on these two commandments" (Matthew 22:36-40).

Q. Where can one find Jesus' statement that a person is either with Him or against Him?

A. The statement is, "Whoever is not with me is against me, and whoever does not gather with me scatters," and it can be found in Matthew 12:30 or Luke 11:23. Jesus was responding to the Pharisees who had accused Him of driving out demons "only by the power of Beelzebul, the prince of demons" (Matthew 12:24). He said that if this were true, Satan would be divided against himself and would be destroying his own kingdom.

Q. In that same encounter, Jesus said that "every sin and blasphemy will be forgiven people, but blasphemy against the Spirit will not be forgiven" (Matthew 12:31). What did He mean by that?

A. By blasphemy against the Spirit Jesus was talking about attributing to Satan what is the work of the Holy Spirit, i.e., casting out demons. He was also referring to the sin of final impenitence, which is the obstinate rejection of God's mercy and love, even at the moment of death. While a person who is truly sorry for sin will always be pardoned, the person our Lord was talking about does not even seek pardon and completely and finally rejects the assistance the Holy Spirit offers to turn that person away from evil and back to God.

In his encyclical "On the Holy Spirit in the Life of the Church and the World" *(Dominum et Vivificantem)*, Pope John Paul II explained further:

"Blasphemy against the Holy Spirit, then, is the sin committed by the person who claims to have a 'right' to persist in evil - in any sin at all - and who thus rejects Redemption. One closes oneself up in sin, thus making impossible one's conversion, and consequently the remission of sins, which one considers not essential or not important for one's life.

"This is a state of spiritual ruin because blasphemy against the Holy Spirit does not allow one to escape from one's self-imposed imprisonment and open oneself to the divine sources of the purification of consciences and of the remission of sins" (n. 46).

Q. How do we respond to those who are living objectively immoral lives but who say that they believe in Jesus and that they are good persons?

A. Perhaps by asking them exactly what constitutes a "good person" and then by comparing their answer with the one that Jesus gave to the rich young man in the Gospels about keeping the Ten Commandments.

A Catholic who deliberately stays away from Mass commits a grave sin. A Catholic who is involved in adultery or fornication commits a grave sin. One cannot repeatedly sin gravely against the law of God and still be a good person. Oh, they may be nice to their family and their friends, they may coach youth sports, they may give to charitable causes, and many who know them would take note of all these good actions and classify them as good persons.

But aren't they like the scribes and Pharisees in the Gospels? To whom Jesus said: "You are like whitewashed tombs, which appear beautiful on the outside, but inside are full of dead men's bones and every kind of filth. Even so, on the outside you appear righteous, but inside you are filled with hypocrisy and evildoing" (Matthew 23:27-28).

Pretty harsh language, huh? The kind of talk that those who make up their own religious rules don't want to hear. They want a Jesus whose strongest words are, "Love one another." What these "good persons" forget is that love of neighbor is the second of the two great commandments. The first and the greatest, Jesus said, is, "You shall love the Lord, your God, with all your heart, with all your soul, and with all your mind" (Matthew 22:37).

Persons who truly love God put God first in their lives and avoid committing grave sins. And if they should fall into mortal sin, they go to Confession and seek God's forgiveness. They don't try to excuse or rationalize their sinful behavior by saying things like, "Jesus wants me to be happy." The reply to that is, no, Jesus wants you to be holy. True happiness comes from loving and serving God with all one's heart, soul, and mind.

In a lengthy commentary on Jesus' dialogue with the rich young man, Pope John Paul II said that "the answer to the question, 'What good must I do to have eternal life?' can only be found by turning one's mind and heart to the 'One' who is good: 'No one is good but God alone' (Mk 10:18; cf. Lk 18:19). Only God can answer the question about what is good, because he is the Good itself" (*Veritatis Splendor*, n. 9). The Holy Father said that "people today need to turn to Christ once again in order to receive from him the answer to their questions about what is good and what is evil. Christ is the Teacher, the Risen One who has life in himself and who is always present in his Church and in the world" (n. 8).

So when trying to be a good person, one must look to God, who is Good itself, and model oneself after Him. One must listen to Christ and to His Church. One must keep the Commandments, all ten of them, and strive to overcome all tendencies toward hypocrisy and evildoing. Then it will be clear what St. Augustine meant when he said to God, "You have made us for yourself, and our heart is restless until it rests in you."

Q. Are there places in the Gospels where Jesus specifies actions that are sinful?

A. One place is the Sermon on the Mount (cf. Matthew 5-7) and another place is chapter 7 of Mark, where Jesus was talking about some of the things that defile a person: "Wicked designs come from the deep recesses of the heart; acts of fornication, theft, murder, adulterous conduct, greed, maliciousness, deceit, sensuality, envy, blasphemy, arrogance, an obtuse spirit. All these evils come from within and render a man impure" (Mark 7:21-23).

Q. But isn't it wrong to criticize the immoral actions of others since Jesus said that we are not to judge others?

A. Suppose you go outside and find that your car has been stolen, would you refrain from calling the police because that would be judgmental? Of course not. That doesn't make any sense. Nor does it make sense to refuse to say that certain actions - murder, abortion, racism, adultery, fornication, missing Mass deliberately on Sunday - are wrong. Yes, it would be wrong to judge the sinner because only God knows our motives for doing wrong, and we should leave that judgment up to Him, but it is not wrong to judge the sin.

If Jesus didn't want us to criticize immoral behavior, then why did He say in Matthew 18 that if a person sins, speak to him about his sin; if he won't listen, get one or two others to talk to him; if he won't listen to them, refer him to the Church; if he refuses to listen to the Church, then treat him as an outcast?

Remember that the first Spiritual Work of Mercy is to "admonish the sinner." That's right, warning a person away from sin is a work of mercy and love. Remember, too, that the Lord told Ezekiel (chapter 3) that if he warned the wicked man about his sins and the man ignored the warning and died in his sins, Ezekiel would have saved his own life; but if he did not warn the wicked man and he died in his sins, Ezekiel would be held responsible for the man's death.

Likewise, James says in his letter that anyone who brings a sinner back from the error of his ways will save his own soul from death and will cover a multitude of sins (cf. James 5:20).

The Sermon on the Mount

Chapter 7

The Words of Our Lord

Q. Jesus told us not to call anyone on earth "father," so why do we call priests "father"?

A. If we consider the context of our Lord's remarks, we see that He was denouncing the Pharisees not for using the titles of "rabbi," or "father," or "teacher," but rather for building up a cult of superiority around themselves, for requiring the people to perform hard tasks while avoiding such works themselves. Instead of helping to lighten the burdens on the people, the Pharisees were busy seeking places of honor at banquets, in the synagogues, and in the marketplace.

So Jesus told them to avoid being called " 'Rabbi.' You have but one teacher, and you are all brothers. Call no one on earth your father; you have but one Father in heaven. Do not be called 'Master'; you have but one master, the Messiah" (Matthew 23:8-10). He told them that "the greatest among you must be your servant. Whoever exalts himself will be humbled; but whoever humbles himself will be exalted" (Matthew 23:11-12).

What our Lord was doing was using hyperbole, engaging in extravagant speech to make a point. He was not ruling out the use of such titles (what else are we to call our male parent or the one who instructs our children in school?), but was criticizing the Pharisees for abusing the authority attached to these titles, for proudly setting up themselves, instead of God, as the ultimate authority.

That Christ was not forbidding the use of the title "father" on earth is clear from its use by those in the early Church. For example, when Stephen was brought in before the Sanhedrin, he addressed the members of the ruling council as "my brothers and fathers" (Acts 7:2). In his first letter, John said, "I am writing to you, fathers, because you know him who is from the beginning" (1 John 2:13). And Paul had no problem with being considered as a spiritual father to the people of Corinth: "I am writing you this not to shame you, but to admonish you as my beloved children. Even if you should have countless guides to Christ, yet you do not have many fathers, for I became your father in Christ Jesus through the gospel" (1 Corinthians 4:14-15).

Q. What did Jesus mean by saying that He had other sheep that did not belong to His fold (cf. John 10:16)?

A. In talking about His role as the Good Shepherd, who will lay down his life for his sheep and whose sheep will hear his voice and follow him, Jesus was referring to the Gentiles, to all those who are not Jews. The mission of Jesus is to bring all people into His Church so that one day there will be one Church and one shepherd, Christ Himself.

Q. What did Jesus mean when He said that there were many dwelling places in His Father's house (cf. John 14:2)?

A. Speaking to the Apostles at the Last Supper, Jesus was explaining that not all those in Heaven will enjoy the same degree of happiness there. Although each person will be perfectly happy in knowing and loving God, and will have all the joy that he or she can bear, our Lord was saying that the degree of happiness will vary according to the life we lived on earth.

Talking to the Corinthians about our resurrected bodies, St. Paul said that "there are both heavenly bodies and earthly bodies, but the brightness of the heavenly is one kind and that of the earthly another. The brightness of the sun is one kind, the brightness of the moon another, and the brightness of the stars another. For star differs from star in brightness. So also is the resurrection of the dead" (1 Corinthians 15:40-42).

In other words, those who loved God ardently on earth, who bore trials and crosses patiently, and who seldom offended

God through sin will have a higher degree of happiness in Heaven than those who led sinful lives but turned back to God and saved their souls. Again in the words of Paul: "Whoever sows sparingly will also reap sparingly, and whoever sows bountifully will also reap bountifully" (2 Corinthians 9:6).

Q. In the Our Father that Jesus taught us, we ask God not to lead us into temptation, but why would God do something like that?
A. The first thing that must be said about this petition is that God tempts no one, nor does He let us be tempted beyond our ability to resist. St. James says that "no one experiencing temptation should say, 'I am being tempted by God'; for God is not subject to temptation to evil, and he himself tempts no one. Rather, each person is tempted when he is lured and enticed by his own desire" (James 1:13-14). And St. Paul says in 1st Corinthians that "God is faithful and will not let you be tried beyond your strength; but with the trial he will also provide a way out, so that you may be able to bear it" (10:13).

So what we are really asking in this petition is for God not to let us yield to temptation, not to let us take the way that leads to sin, to distinguish between trials that are necessary for our spiritual growth and temptations that can lead us to sin and spiritual death. This is clearer in St. Luke's version of the Our Father, where our Lord prays, "... and do not subject us to the final test" (11:4).

What is **temptation**? It means an invitation to commit a sin. The temptation itself is not a sin; we must give in to the temptation and commit the evil act in order to sin. Where do temptations come from? The Church has traditionally taught that the three sources of temptation are the world, the flesh, and the Devil. By the world we mean bad companions, movies, TV, the Internet, music, books, magazines, etc. One would have to be blind and deaf not to be exposed to temptations these days.

By the flesh we mean our inclination toward evil that is a result of Original Sin (the theologians call it **concupiscence**). Although Baptism took away that sin, its effects remain with us all our lives in that our minds are sometimes darkened and our wills are sometimes weakened, so that we make bad choices. St. Paul described this condition well when he wrote: "For I do not do the good I want, but I do the evil I do not want" (Romans 7:19). The way to overcome this attraction to evil is prayer and the Sacraments.

By the Devil we mean that evil spirit who, in the words of St. Peter, prowls about the world "like a roaring lion looking for [someone] to devour" (1 Peter 5:8). Jesus had his own battles with the Devil, particularly after He had prayed and fasted for forty days in the desert, and Satan offered him the same three temptations that we face constantly - temptations to pleasure, to pride, and to power (cf. Matthew 4:1-11).

Satan wasn't sure who Jesus was because he prefaced each temptation with the words, "If you are the Son of God." He tempted the hungry Jesus to seek the pleasure of eating by changing stones into bread, but the Lord replied that " 'one does not live by bread alone,/ but by every word that comes forth/ from the mouth of God' " (4:4).

Satan tempted Christ to pride in gaining fame and prestige by throwing Himself down from the top of the Temple and letting His angels rescue Him, but Jesus said, "Again it is written, 'You shall not put the Lord, your God, to the test' " (4:7).

The Devil then tempted Christ to power by showing Him all the kingdoms of the world and promising to give all of them to Him if He would bow down to the Evil One. To which Jesus replied, "Get away, Satan! It is written: 'The Lord, your God, shall you worship/ and him alone shall you serve' " (4:10).

By including this petition in the Our Father, Jesus unites us to His battle with temptation, and He urges us to be vigilant and to persevere. When we pray this petition, says

Pope Benedict in his book *Jesus of Nazareth*, we are saying to God: "I know that I need trials so that my nature can be purified. When you decide to send me these trials, when you give evil some room to maneuver ... then please remember that my strength only goes so far. Don't overestimate my capacity. Don't set too wide the boundaries within which I may be tempted, and be close to me with your protecting hand when it becomes too much for me" (p. 163).

Q. How are we to understand Jesus' statement about His coming to earth to spread not peace but division among families?

A. First, here are the words of our Lord as they can be found in two of the Gospels: "Do you think that I have come to establish peace on the earth? No, I tell you, but rather division. From now on a household of five will be divided, three against two and two against three; a father will be divided against his son and a son against his father, a mother against her daughter and a daughter against her mother, a mother-in-law against her daughter-in-law and a daughter-in-law against her mother-in-law" (Luke 12:51-53; see also Matthew 10:34-38).

Jesus is not saying that He wants to break up families, but rather that there will inevitably be divisions in families among those who want to keep His teachings and follow His law and those who don't. For example, there could be splits between a father and son over Mass attendance or moving in with a girl friend, or between a mother and daughter over divorce and remarriage, or between a mother-in-law and daughter-in-law over abortion.

Jesus does not desire these divisions, of course, but He is reminding us that they are inevitable unless all members of a family conform their lives to His divine plan. "Whoever loves father and mother more than me is not worthy of me," Jesus said, "and whoever loves son or daughter more than me is not worthy of me; and whoever does not take up his cross and follow after me is not worthy of me" (Matthew 10:37-38).

Q. What point was Jesus trying to make in the incident involving Martha and Mary when Jesus visited their house?

A. As St. Luke tells the story in his Gospel, Martha was busy waiting on Jesus, getting a meal ready, while Mary sat at His feet listening to Him. When Martha complained to Jesus and asked Him to tell Mary to help her, Christ said, "Martha, Martha, you are anxious and worried about many things. There is need of only one thing. Mary has chosen the better part and it will not be taken from her" (Luke 10:41-42).

Jesus was not saying that Martha had chosen something bad; after all hospitality to one's visitors is a good thing. What He was saying was that sitting at His feet was not mere laziness on Mary's part, but rather the highest form of activity, absorbing the words of the Lord and seeking greater holiness.

An even more striking example of the importance of being attentive to the word of God can be found in chapter 11 of Luke, where a woman called out to Jesus, "Blessed is the womb that carried you and the breasts at which you nursed." The Lord replied, "Rather, blessed are those who hear the word of God and observe it" (Luke 11:27-28).

This was certainly not a rebuke of His mother, who had been exceedingly blessed in carrying the Christ Child in her womb, but it was a reminder that paying attention to God and putting His words into practice are of greater importance than one's biological relationship with Jesus.

Q. Why did Jesus do so much of His teaching in parables? Why didn't He speak plainly to the people?

A. It was after Jesus told the parable of the sower going out to plant seed (Mark 4:3-9) - on the pathway, on rocky ground, among thorns, and finally on rich soil - that the disciples questioned Him about this method of teaching. Jesus told them that "the mystery of the kingdom of God has been granted to you. But to those outside everything comes in parables, so that/ 'they may look and see but not perceive,/ and hear and listen but not understand,/ in order that they may not be converted/ and be forgiven' " (Mark 4:11-12).

If we recall that Jesus faced considerable unbelief and hostility in His ministry, we can see the need for presenting the kingdom in one way to the disbelieving crowd (through parables, such as the sower and the seed in this case), and in another way to the disciples (through explanation of the parables). The reason for the different approaches was that the disciples were well-disposed by faith to accept the teachings of Jesus, while the crowds were not. Their hearts were still hardened and their minds were still darkened to an understanding of the reign of God, and they would require a more gradual unveiling of the mystery of the kingdom.

Jesus was a master at using ordinary events and people to illustrate profound spiritual truths, but He had to tread cautiously with the people because they were not ready for the truth about His real identity. They were expecting a Messiah who would be a warrior king, not a "suffering servant."

Jesus wants understanding, acceptance, and healing, but only when we have set aside all obstacles and are truly open to His love. Then the moral lessons hidden in the parables will be fully revealed to us. For a wonderful treatment of the parables of our Lord, see chapter seven of Pope Benedict's book *Jesus of Nazareth*.

Q. How do we answer the objection that Jesus was wrong in the parable of the mustard seed (cf. Matthew 13:31-32) when He said that it was the smallest seed there is?

A. The answer is that Jesus was not speaking in absolute terms, but in relative terms regarding the size of the plant that can grow to eight or ten feet from such a tiny seed. He was teaching a religious lesson about the growth of His kingdom, not a botany lesson. Jesus was using an inexact comparison to make a point, just as we often do. For example, we frequently talk about the sun rising in the morning, but that's an error since the sun does not rise; it's the rotation of the earth that makes the sun appear to be rising.

Q. So Jesus was not teaching us an economics lesson in the story of the workers in the vineyard (Matthew 20:1-16), where the man who only worked one hour late in the day was paid the same as the one who worked all day long?

A. That is correct. Jesus was illustrating the mercy of God in making eternal salvation available to all - those who have been faithful all their lives and those who turned back to God late in life. As mentioned by St. Paul, those who served God longer and more constantly on earth will enjoy greater happiness in Heaven (cf. 2 Corinthians 9:6). But salvation will be granted even to souls with lesser qualifications, provided they died free from all mortal sin.

Jesus was directing this parable to the Pharisees, those whom St. Luke said "were convinced of their own righteousness and despised everyone else" (Luke 18:9). Remember the parable about the Pharisee and the tax collector praying in the Temple (Luke 18:9-14). The Pharisee was boasting of his righteousness and looking scornfully at the tax collector beating his breast and begging for God's mercy. "I tell you," said Jesus, "the latter went home justified, not the former; for everyone who exalts himself will be humbled, and the one who humbles himself will be exalted" (Luke 18:14).

Q. Why did Jesus cause a fig tree to wither and die? That seems like a strange thing to do.

A. On the way to Jerusalem one day, Jesus saw a fig tree with leaves on it and walked over to get some figs to eat. When

He saw that there were no figs on the tree, He said, "May no one ever eat of your fruit again!" (Mark 11:14). On the following day, when Jesus and the Apostles passed by the tree, it had withered and died. What was the point of this action, especially when Mark points out that it was not the time of the year for figs, a fact that Jesus must have known?

This was a parable in action. Jesus was comparing the fig tree with the Chosen People. They had been waiting for centuries for the Messiah, but when He came they did not recognize Him, and they would soon put Him to death. They put on an outward show of religion, just as the fig tree put on an outward show of fruitfulness, but they were spiritually barren on the inside, just as the tree was physically barren.

The lesson has application in our own time as well. How many today put on an outward show of religiosity, but their hearts are far from God? We know with much more certainty today that Jesus is the Messiah, but how many of us live as if He had never come? Perhaps these are the people James was talking about when he said that "faith without works is dead" (James 2:26), just as a fig tree without fruit is dead.

Q. Wasn't it rather extreme for Jesus to say that if one's eye or hand leads one into sin, it would better to gouge out that eye or cut off that hand rather than have one's entire body cast into Hell (cf. Matthew 5:29-30)?

A. Our Lord's words are not to be taken literally, of course, since mutilation of one's body is a sin. Once again, Jesus was using hyperbole or extravagant speech to make a point. He was saying that eternal damnation is such a terrible punishment that a person would be better off in the long run to gouge out an eye or cut off a hand and go through life maimed rather than let that eye or hand lead to an eternity in Hell. Christ was not advocating such an extreme course of action, but He was trying to warn His listeners of the dire consequences of a life of deliberate unforgiven sin.

Q. Was it also hyperbole when Jesus said, "If anyone comes to me without hating his father and mother, wife and children, brothers and sisters, and even his own life, he cannot be my disciple" (Luke 14:26)?

A. Yes. Jesus didn't mean "hate" in the usual sense of despising someone; rather He was saying, "If you do not love me more than family members, then you cannot be my disciple." We are certainly to love family members, but to love them less than we love Jesus. They must always take second place to the Lord if we are to be His true disciples.

Q. On the question of divorce, why does Jesus apparently soften His opposition to it in Matthew 5:32, when He says that "whoever divorces his wife (unless the marriage is unlawful) causes her to commit adultery, and whoever marries a divorced woman commits adultery"?

A. This is the so-called "Matthean exception," which is not really an exception at all, since Jesus clearly condemned divorce in other places (cf. Mark 10:2-12 and Luke 16:18). The key to understanding this passage is the word *porneia*, which can be translated as an unlawful sexual union. In the community to which Matthew was writing, there were persons who appeared to be married, but were actually in illicit unions according to the Mosaic law (cf. Leviticus 18:6-18), which forbade marriages between persons of certain blood and/or legal relationships.

These "marriages," which were regarded as incestuous, were permitted by some rabbis who allowed Gentile converts to Judaism to remain in them. Matthew's exception is opposed to allowing such a status for Gentile converts to Christianity. So the clause is not an exception to the absolute prohibition of divorce when the marriage is lawfully contracted.

Q. Jesus tells us to love our enemies (Luke 6:27) and to offer no resistance to an evil person (cf. Matthew 5:39). And yet

the *Catechism of the Catholic Church* seems to contradict Jesus by affirming our right to self-defense, including the use of lethal means, to defeat an evil aggressor (cf. n. 2264). In light of this, how are we to respond to something like the September 11th attacks on the World Trade Center in New York and on the Pentagon?

A. The Christian response to atrocities like September 11th should include both love of enemies, which means praying for their conversion of heart and mind, and steps to protect ourselves from future terrorist attacks. Jesus' remark about offering no resistance to one who is evil applies to individuals, who may heroically "turn the other cheek," as did many martyrs. However, He did not mean that states or governments should not resist evil since that would endanger the lives of the people who depend on them for protection from foreign and domestic enemies.

While legitimate defense is the right of the individual because, in the words of St. Thomas Aquinas, "one is bound to take more care of one's own life than of another's," the *Catechism* says that right becomes "a grave duty for one who is responsible for the lives of others. The defense of the common good requires that an unjust aggressor be rendered unable to cause harm. For this reason, those who legitimately hold authority also have the right to use arms to repel aggressors against the civil community entrusted to their responsibility" (n. 2265).

Although Jesus was in contact with soldiers during His public life - in fact, He cured the servant of one of them and praised the centurion's faith (cf. Matthew 8:10), and another soldier, standing at the Cross on Good Friday, said after Christ had expired, "Truly this man was the Son of God!" (Mark 15:39) - there is no record of Jesus condemning military service, even though many of the soldiers whom He encountered were engaged in oppressing the Jewish people.

In his World Day of Peace message in 1984, Pope John

Paul II upheld "the principle of legitimate defense" and rejected pacifism. He said that a "person who deeply desires peace rejects any kind of pacifism, which is cowardice, or the simple preservation of tranquility. In fact, those who are tempted to impose their domination will always encounter the resistance of intelligent and courageous men and women, prepared to defend freedom in order to promote justice."

Addressing Italian soldiers in 1989, the Holy Father said that "the military profession is defined as the task of defending the justice and freedom of the nation, and consequently of contributing to the tranquility and peace of the entire world." He said that peace must be defended because "it is out of love of neighbor, of one's loved ones, of the weakest and most defenseless, as well as the love of the spiritual values and traditions of one's nation, that one must agree to self-sacrifice, to struggle, and even to give up one's life, should it be necessary."

Q. Jesus said that anyone who is angry with his brother will be liable to judgment (cf. Matthew 5:22). Does that mean that all forms of anger are sinful, and that there is no such thing as righteous anger in a human being?

A. The glossary at the back of the *Catechism* defines anger as "an emotion which is not in itself wrong, but which, when it is not controlled by reason or hardens into resentment and hate, becomes one of the seven capital sins. Christ taught that anger is an offense against the fifth commandment."

Thus, there are those all-too-frequent occasions when anger is not controlled by reason and when it turns into resentment and hate and seeks revenge on the object of one's anger. Humans flawed by Original Sin are not usually able to handle their righteous indignation in the correct way in order to keep it from becoming a mortal sin. But are there times when righteous anger is appropriate?

St. Paul remarked on the distinction between righteous

indignation and sinful anger when he said, "Be angry but do not sin" (Ephesians 4:26). In other words, when there is a just reason for indignation, don't go to the extreme of committing sin by becoming furious over small matters or by venting rage on a person. St. Paul offers this additional advice:

"Do not repay anyone evil for evil; be concerned for what is noble in the sight of all. If possible, on your part, live at peace with all. Beloved, do not look for revenge but leave room for the wrath; for it is written, 'Vengeance is mine, I will repay, says the Lord' " (Romans 12:17-19).

So when is righteous anger justified? How about when parents or a teacher must confront a child who has been involved in serious wrongdoing? Or when a woman has to refuse immoral advances by a man? Or when someone asks you to lie about the actions of a superior to cause the superior to lose his job? Such indignation is good if it helps one to ward off harm and if it prevents one from falling into sin. Was righteous anger the proper response to the terrorist attacks on the Pentagon and the World Trade Center in 2001? Reasonable and moral persons would say yes.

We must remember, however, that there is a fine line between just and unjust anger, and we must be cautious not to cross that line. St. Francis de Sales gave some good advice when he was asked how he kept so calm in the face of hostility. "I have made an agreement with my tongue," he said, "never to say a word while my heart is excited." He is echoed by moral theologian Germain Grisez in his book *Living a Christian Life*:

"Someone feeling even justifiable anger should regain his or her composure before offering an admonition, so that it can be given humbly, gently, kindly, and peaceably - in a word, as a true work of mercy. Admonition need not always be done by words. Gestures, actions, or a manner that goads another's conscience are sometimes more effective. Even when words are appropriate, questions should come before assertions:

'Question a friend; perhaps he did not do it;
or if he did, so that he may not do it again.
Question a neighbor; perhaps he did not say it;
or if he said it, so that he may not repeat it'
(Sir 19:12-13).

"Questions incite reflection, and so are more likely than assertion to be effective. They also reflect the reality that in admonishing one always addresses an apparent sinner whose internal guilt one cannot judge. It also is important to choose the right time and place for an admonition; but this should not become an excuse for evading the responsibility by requiring an ideal situation that will never occur" (p. 231).

Q. Jesus told us "not to perform righteous deeds in order that people may see them .... But when you fast, anoint your head and wash your face, so that you may not appear to others to be fasting, except to your Father who is hidden. And your Father who sees what is hidden will repay you" (Matthew 6:1, 17-18). But what about going out in public with ashes on our foreheads on Ash Wednesday?

A. Jesus is not condemning the performance of religious acts and duties in public, but rather the attitude of performing them to impress other people, instead of to serve God. Recall that in Matthew 23:5, He condemned those Pharisees whose "works are performed to be seen. They widen their phylacteries and lengthen their tassels" (Phylacteries were small capsules containing miniature scrolls with Bible verses on them. They were strapped either to the forehead or to the upper left arm and were worn in public.)

If a person today were to get ashes just to impress other people, that would be a phony display of piety, instead of the real thing. On the other hand, if one were to display the ashes with an attitude of genuine piety, then the act might give good example to others and might even serve as an actual grace that could change the heart of someone who had fallen away from the Faith.

Recall the words of Jesus that present the positive side of this question: "Your light must shine before others, that they may see your good deeds and glorify your heavenly Father" (Matthew 5:16).

Jesus and His Agony in the Garden

Chapter 8

Jesus' Passion, Death, and Resurrection

Q. Did Jesus, in the Garden of Gethsemane and on the Cross, know the sins for which He was giving His life?

A. Yes. God's foreknowledge of us and our actions is attested to in Scripture, for example, in Psalm 139:13-16: "You formed my inmost being;/ you knit me in my mother's womb./ I praise you, so wonderfully you made me;/ wonderful are your works!/ My very self you knew;/ my bones were not hidden from you,/ When I was being made in secret,/ fashioned as in the depths of the earth./ Your eyes foresaw my actions;/ in your book all are written down;/ my days were shaped, before one came to be."

In his *Life of Christ*, Archbishop Fulton J. Sheen also provided some insight into how our sins caused Christ to suffer during His agony in the Garden of Gethsemane, how the Lord had to take upon His sinless shoulders all the sins that had been committed from the time of Adam until the end of the world, causing Him a mental anguish that may have been worse than the physical pains of the Cross. Here is how Archbishop Sheen put it:

> "He saw the betrayals of future Judases, the sins of heresy that would rend Christ's Mystical Body; the sins of the Communists who could not drive God from the heavens but would drive His ambassadors from the earth; He saw the broken marriage vows, lies, slanders, adulteries, murders, apostasies - all these crimes were thrust into His own hands, as if He had committed them. Evil desires lay upon His heart, as if He Himself had given them birth. Lies and schisms rested on His mind, as if He Himself had conceived them. Blasphemies seemed to be on His lips, as if He had spoken them.

"From the North, South, East, and West, the foul miasma of the world's sins rushed upon Him like a flood; Samson-like, He reached up and pulled the whole guilt of the world upon Himself as if He were guilty, paying for the debt in our name, so that we might once more have access to the Father. He was, so to speak, mentally preparing Himself for the great sacrifice, laying upon His sinless soul the sins of a guilty world. To most men, the burden of sin is as natural as the clothes they wear, but to Him the touch of that which men take so easily was the veriest agony" (Popular Library edition, p. 375).

Q. If the Apostles were asleep in the Garden of Gethsemane, how could they have known what Jesus said? Or how could they know the words that were said during His trials or His exchange with Pontius Pilate, the Roman governor?

A. First of all, the Apostles knew what Jesus had said in the Garden because they had not yet fallen asleep. Recall that the Lord told them to stay awake and keep watch with Him. He then walked a short distance away and prostrated himself in prayer, saying, "My Father, if it is possible, let this cup pass from me" (Matthew 26:39). Peter, James, and John were surely still awake for this utterance, but then drifted off to sleep as Jesus continued to pray.

Second, it seems that all of the dialogue between Jesus and Pilate took place in public, whether inside or outside the praetorium (place of judgment), so there were plenty of listeners to what was said. We sometimes think of the Apostles and disciples as being outsiders, but there are hints in the Gospels that some of them were well-known to the religious and civil leaders. For example, one of Jesus' disciples (probably John) is described as an "acquaintance of the high priest" who was able to get Peter inside the courtyard while Jesus was being interrogated by Annas (cf. John 18:16).

In another place, Joanna, one of the women who ministered to the needs of Jesus and the Twelve, is described as the wife of King Herod's steward Chuza (Luke 8:3), so the disciples had connections in Herod's inner circle. We also know that two members of the Sanhedrin - Nicodemus and Joseph of Arimathea - were sympathizers of Jesus who would have reported on what happened there.

Finally, we know that our Lord spent forty days with the Apostles between the Resurrection and the Ascension, providing them with information that was necessary for them to spread His message first in oral and then in written form. It is not difficult to imagine Peter, James, and John asking Christ, "Lord, tell us what happened in the Garden while we were sleeping and during your trials before the Sanhedrin and Pilate."

Q. In the Stations of the Cross, a woman named Veronica is mentioned as having given our Lord a veil to wipe His bloody face, and when He handed the cloth back to her, His face was painted in blood on the veil. Why is this not mentioned in the Gospels, and does that cloth still exist?

A. It is true that Veronica is not mentioned in any of the four Gospel accounts of Christ's walk to Calvary. The incident has come down to us through oral Tradition, and the woman is called Veronica because the Latin words for the "true image" that appeared on her veil are *vera icon.*

The icon which is thought to be Veronica's veil is kept at the Sanctuary of the Holy Face in Manoppello, Italy, about 120 miles from Rome. During a visit to the shrine in 2006, Pope Benedict XVI said that "looking for Jesus' face must be the yearning of all Christians," that for those who persevere in the search, Christ "will be there at the end of our earthly pilgrimage," and that all must imitate the saints in recognizing the face of Jesus in their brothers and sisters, "especially the poorest and those most in need."

The Holy Father prayed for several minutes before the protective glass case that houses the 7-inch-by-9.5-inch transparent veil that portrays the image of a man with long hair and a beard. Studies have found that no paints or pigments were used to create the image.

Q. Can you explain what Jesus meant when He told the women on the way to Calvary, "... if these things are done when the wood is green what will happen when it is dry?" (Luke 23:31)?

A. In His comments to the women of Jerusalem who were weeping over Him, Jesus first warned them of the calamities to come and then said the quoted words. He was telling them that if the innocent, like Himself, must undergo many sufferings, those guilty of sin would be even more severely punished.

Q. Why was it necessary for Jesus to die in such a brutal way? Couldn't He have redeemed us by a simple act of His will?

A. One answer might be that we can learn so much more about God and His incredible love for us from the Passion and Death of Jesus than we could ever have learned if God had simply pardoned us. In volume three of their compendium entitled *Radio Replies*, Frs. Leslie Rumble and Charles Carty offered this explanation:

> "Had God willed it, Christ could have saved us without undergoing so much suffering, But God willed otherwise, and Jesus undertook to satisfy for human nature in human nature, and in generous measure indeed. Nor was His long-drawn-out and intense Passion superfluous. He thus made superabundant satisfaction for our sins, gave us an extreme manifestation of His love for us, set us an example of almost every virtue in almost every possible

trial, and intensified the motives why those who profess to believe in Him should refrain from further sin. Thus Christ made essential reparation by His death, and circumstantial reparation by enduring all types of penalties deserved by the various sins of men" (p. 173).

Q. How do you answer those who say that they did not go to see *The Passion of the Christ* because of the film's "gratuitous violence"? Is this an accurate assessment of the movie?

A. Having seen the film twice, we don't think so. "Gratuitous" means uncalled for or unwarranted, but is *The Passion of the Christ* unnecessarily violent? Or did director Mel Gibson accurately portray what really happened to our Lord? Did Jesus really undergo such a bloody scourging, crowning with thorns, and nailing to the cross? Well, yes, He did. Granted, the Gospels give very few details about the Passion of Christ, but historians who have studied Roman methods of execution, and doctors who have explained the medical and physiological effects of scourging and crucifixion, provide solid evidence that Gibson did not exaggerate the cruelties inflicted on Jesus (cf. the book *A Doctor at Calvary* by Pierre Barbet, a French surgeon who devoted many years to studying the Passion).

Take the scourging of our Lord, for example. The usual punishment was 39 lashes, but doctors who have studied the scourge marks on the Man whose image appears on the Shroud of Turin, which many believe to be the burial cloth of Jesus, estimate that He was struck about 120 times. The whips that were used in the movie, tipped with pieces of metal designed to tear holes in human flesh, are just like those used by the Romans, and they are capable of causing horrendous damage to the human body.

Here is a description of scourging that appeared in Giuseppe Ricciotti's *Life of Christ*:

"Usually whoever underwent the Roman scourging was reduced to a sickening and terrifying monstrosity. At the first blows the neck, back, hips, arms, and legs grew livid, and then became streaked with bluish welts and swollen bruises; then the skin and muscles were gradually lacerated, the blood vessels burst and blood spurted everywhere, till finally the prisoner, every one of his features disfigured, was nothing but a bleeding mass of flesh. Very often he fainted under the blows, and sometimes he died" (p. 621).

So the portrayal of the sufferings of Christ in the film was not exaggerated. He really was "nothing but a bleeding mass of flesh." Add to that the crowning with long, sharp thorns that were pounded into His scalp; carrying a cross that might have weighed 75 or 80 pounds nearly half a mile; the hammering of nails through His hands and feet that caused excruciating pain; and three hours of cramping muscles and breathing agonies on the Cross before He finally suffocated to death, and you have a true picture of what Jesus willingly endured to ransom us from our sins.

Every one of those wounds was Christ's way of atoning for all the sins from Adam to the end of the world - sins of the head (lustful, envious, and hateful thoughts), sins of the body (fornication, adultery, masturbation, homosexual acts), sins of the hands and feet (abortion, murder, theft, gluttony, prostitution, slavery). There was no sin, past, present, or future, that Jesus did not take on His sinless shoulders and for which He did not shed blood. And don't forget His mental agony, the knowledge that His suffering and death would be in vain for those who would never repent of their sins and would wind up in Hell.

A sterile and cleaned-up version of the Sorrowful Mysteries of the rosary would not have had nearly the impact on viewers that *The Passion of the Christ* had. Let us pray that Mel Gibson's truthful and stunning depiction of the last hours in the life of Christ will motivate millions of people to repent of their sins and believe in the Gospel of Jesus.

Q. Why do Catholics have a cross with the body of Jesus on it, instead of just a plain cross. If Jesus is risen, why show Him on the Cross?

A. Why do we show Jesus as a baby in the manger long after He has grown up? Because we want to remember that particular moment when the Son of God visibly became man. So, too, we use a crucifix because we want to remember that particular moment when the Son of God shed His blood for our salvation.

How can Catholics play down the Crucifixion when Jesus and St. Paul emphasized it so strongly? Jesus often talked about His followers taking up their cross (Matthew 16:24). He said that "when I am lifted up from the earth [on the Cross], I will draw everyone to myself" (John 12:32). And so millions have been drawn to follow Christ by praying before a crucifix and meditating on the suffering that He endured for us and for our salvation.

"I resolved to know nothing while I was with you except Jesus Christ, and him crucified," Paul told the people of Corinth (1 Corinthians 2:2). Earlier in the same letter, the Apostle said: "For Jews demand signs and Greeks look for wisdom, but we proclaim Christ crucified, a stumbling block to Jews and foolishness to Gentiles, but to those who are called, Jews and Greeks alike, Christ the power of God and the wisdom of God" (1:22-24).

Paul talked about the evidence for the Resurrection in chapter 15 of 1st Corinthians, and the importance of Christ's rising from the dead and what it will mean to us at the end of the world, but he gave more emphasis to the death of Jesus, who "humbled himself,/ becoming obedient to death,/ even death on a cross" (Philippians 2:8). Paul said that he was "always carrying about in the body the dying of Jesus" (2 Corinthians 4:10), and he expressed the hope that "the cross of Christ might not be emptied of its meaning" (1 Corinthians 1:17).

What happened on Easter Sunday is supremely important, but every Easter is preceded by a Good Friday, by the greatest act of love and sacrifice in human history. That event cannot have as profound an impact on us if we are looking at a bare cross, but only when we contemplate the five precious wounds of our Lord and Savior. In the words of an unknown poet:

> "Lo! There He hangs, ashened figure - pinioned to the wood./ God grant that I might love Him - even as I should./ I draw a little closer - to touch that face divine./ And then He leans to whisper - 'Ah, foolish child of mine./ If now I should embrace you - my hands would stain you red./ And if I leaned to kiss you - the thorns would pierce your head.' T'was then I learned in meekness - that love demands a price./ T'was then I knew that suffering - is but the kiss of Christ."

Q. What do the letters "INRI" mean?

A. It was the custom of the Romans to place a sign above the head of a person being crucified to indicate the nature of his crime, and thus to forewarn passersby not to engage in such actions themselves, lest they face the same penalty. The sign above Jesus' head was in three languages - Latin, Hebrew, and Greek. In Latin, where the letter "I" is substituted for the letter "J", INRI meant *Iesus Nazarenus Rex Iudaeorum*, or "Jesus of Nazareth, King of the Jews."

It is interesting to note that when the chief priests saw the sign, they complained to Pontius Pilate, "Do not write 'The King of the Jews,' but that he said, 'I am the King of the Jews.' " Pilate answered, "What I have written, I have written" (John 19:21-22).

Q. Didn't Jesus' cry from the Cross, "My God, my God, why have you forsaken me?" (Matthew 27:46), indicate that He had lost faith in His Father?

A. No, it did not. Christ on the Cross knew exactly what He was doing, that He was carrying out the Father's will by offering His life for us. He knew that His sacrifice would not be in vain, but He wanted to experience the deepest depths of desolation and mental agony, as if He had been completely forsaken, so that He could encompass all the loneliness and abandonment of those who have rejected God and could show us the price He was willing to pay for our sins.

Jesus was not giving into despair; He was reciting the second verse of Psalm 22, which begins with cries of anguish and abandonment, but moves on to words of praise and thanksgiving to the God who "has not spurned or disdained/ the misery of this poor wretch,/ Did not turn away from me,/ but heard me when I cried out" (22:25). The Psalm concludes with words of triumph:

> "All the ends of the earth/ will worship and turn to the LORD;/ All the families of nations/ will bow low before you./ ... The generation to come will be told of the/ Lord,/ that they may proclaim to a people yet/ unborn/ the deliverance you have brought" (22:28, 32).

Q. In his account of the Passion of Christ, why is Luke the only evangelist who quotes Jesus' statement to the good thief that "today you will be with me in Paradise" (Luke 23:43)?

A. It's a matter of each evangelist deciding what to include in his particular account of the Passion. Just as if several of those reading this were sent to cover the execution of Christ, all would be in general agreement about what happened, but each would single out certain sayings or incidents that they considered important. We know, for example, that Jesus spoke seven times from the Cross, but if you read Matthew and Mark, you will find only one saying: "My God, my God, why have you forsaken me?"

There are three sayings in Luke and three more in John, so you have to read all four accounts of the Passion to get the full story. John got his information by being the only evangelist at the Cross on Good Friday, and Luke explains in the prologue to his Gospel where he got his information:

> "Since many have undertaken to compile a narrative of the events that have been fulfilled among us, just as those who were eyewitnesses from the beginning and ministers of the word have handed them down to us, I too have decided, after investigating everything accurately anew, to write it down in an orderly sequence" (Luke 1:1-3).

Q. In recent years, medical studies of the Crucifixion of Jesus have concluded that the nails were driven through the wrists of Christ, not the palms of His hands. But in photographs and biographies of Padre Pio and other saints who had the stigmata, the nail marks always appeared in their palms. Why the difference?

A. Because the stigmata have a mystical significance and do not necessarily duplicate the physical location of the five wounds of Christ. This is true, for example, of the wound from the lance, which most authorities place on Jesus' right side, but which some stigmatists have on the left side.

Discussing the wounds in the hands in his classic book *A Doctor at Calvary*, Dr. Pierre Barbet said that "the exact localization of these stigmata is not always the same, but it varies throughout the whole extent of the metacarpal zone, as far as being very near to the wrists. We should come to the conclusion that the stigmatists can give us no information either as to the position or the form of the wounds of the Crucifixion" (p. 105).

As evidence of the spiritual significance of the wounds, Barbet cited stigmatist Theresa Neumann, who told one of her friends: "Do not think that Our Saviour was nailed in the hands, where I have my stigmata. These marks only have a mystical meaning. Jesus must have been fixed more firmly on the Cross" *(Ibid.)*.

Q. Is there a devotion concerning the wounds of Christ, where a person using rosary beads says the following prayers: on the Our Father bead, "Eternal Father, I offer You the wounds of our Lord Jesus Christ to heal the wounds of our souls," and on the Hail Mary bead, "My Jesus, pardon and mercy through the merits of your Holy Wounds"?
A. These prayers were given by Jesus to Sister M. Martha Chambon, a Visitation Order nun in Chambery, France, sometime in the late 1860s. During many visits to Sister Chambon, Jesus granted her contemplation of His five Holy Wounds and gave her power to unite her sufferings with His to bring about release of souls in Purgatory. Here are Christ's words to her:

> "The benefit of the Holy Wounds causes graces to descend from Heaven and the souls in Purgatory to ascend there. Every time you look at the Divine crucified with a pure heart, you will obtain deliverance for five souls from Purgatory, one at each source. If your heart is very pure and well-detached, you will also obtain the same favor at each station in making the Way of the Cross, through the merits of each of my wounds. When you offer my Holy Wounds for sinners, you must not forget to do so for the souls in Purgatory, as there are but few who think of their relief. The Holy Wounds are the treasure of treasures for the souls in Purgatory."

Q. Who is responsible for the death of Jesus - the Jewish leaders of the time, the Romans, or all of us?

A. In Vatican II's "Declaration on the Relationship of the Church to Non-Christian Religions" *(Nostra Aetate),* the Council Fathers said (n. 4) that, according to the testimony of Holy Scripture, "Jerusalem did not recognize the time of her visitation (cf. Lk. 19:44), nor did the Jews in large number accept the gospel; indeed, not a few opposed the spreading of it (cf. Rom. 11:28). Nevertheless, according to the Apostle, the Jews still remain most dear to God because of their fathers, for He does not repent of the gifts He makes nor of the calls He issues (cf. Rom. 11:28-29)."

In the same paragraph of *Nostra Aetate,* the Council Fathers went on to say it is true that "authorities of the Jews and those who followed their lead pressed for the death of Christ (cf. Jn. 19:6); still, what happened in His Passion cannot be blamed upon all the Jews then living, without distinction, nor upon the Jews of today. Although the Church is the new people of God, the Jews should not be presented as repudiated or cursed by God, as if such views followed from the holy Scriptures."

A footnote to the last sentence adds these comments: "As Cardinal Bea and others explained, 'His blood be upon us and upon our children' (Mt. 27:25) is the cry of a Jerusalem crowd that has no right to speak for the whole Jewish people. The severity of Christ's judgment on Jerusalem (Mt. 23:37 ff., etc.) does not suppose or prove collective culpability of the Jewish people for the Crucifixion; that judgment caps a long history of Jerusalem's disobedience to God, crimes against the prophets, etc., and it is a 'type' of the universal, final judgment."

So Vatican II made the necessary distinctions between those Jewish leaders of Jesus' time who pressed for His death and other Jews then living who were not part of the plot. But while assigning blame specifically to those who were guilty, the Council at the same time repudiated "the hatred, persecutions, and displays of anti-Semitism directed against the Jews at any time and from any source," adding that "as the Church has always held and continues to hold, Christ in His boundless love freely underwent His Passion and Death because of the sins of all men, so that all might attain salvation" (n. 4).

A footnote to this sentence refers to the *Catechism of the Council of Trent*, which stated in 1566 that guilt for Christ's death "seems more enormous in us than in the Jews, since according to the testimony of the same Apostle: 'If they had known it, they would never have crucified the Lord of glory' (1 Cor. 2:8); while we, on the contrary, professing to know Him, yet denying Him by our actions, seem in some sort to lay violent hands on Him."

Or as St. Francis of Assisi said, "It is you who have crucified Him and crucify Him still, when you delight in your vices and sins."

Q. What did St. Paul mean in Colossians 1:24, when he said that "in my flesh I am filling up what is lacking in the afflictions of Christ on behalf of his body, which is the church"? What could possibly be lacking in Christ's sufferings?

A. Paul did not mean that Christ's sufferings were not infinitely valuable and sufficient for our redemption, because they were. What the Apostle meant was that we can add our sufferings to those of Christ so that the fruits of His Redemption can be applied to people everywhere. In his letter on suffering (*Salvifici Doloris*), Pope John Paul II dwelt at some length on the meaning of these words of St. Paul. Among other things, the Holy Father said:

"The sufferings of Christ created the good of the world's Redemption. This good in itself is inexhaustible and infinite. No man can add anything to it. But at the same time, in the mystery of the Church as His body, Christ has in a sense opened His own redemptive suffering to all human suffering. Insofar as man becomes a sharer in Christ's sufferings - in any part of the world and at any time in history - to that extent he in his own way completes the suffering through which Christ accomplished the Redemption of the world.

"Does this mean that the Redemption achieved by Christ is not complete? No. It only means that the Redemption, accomplished through satisfactory love, remains always open to all love expressed in human suffering. In this dimension - the dimension of love - the Redemption which has already been completely accomplished is, in a certain sense, constantly being accomplished.

"Christ achieved the Redemption completely and to the very limit; but at the same time He did not bring it to a close. In this redemptive suffering, through which the Redemption of the world was accomplished, Christ opened Himself from the beginning to every human suffering and constantly does so. Yes, it seems to be part of the very essence of Christ's redemptive suffering that this suffering requires to be unceasingly completed" (n. 24).

Q. Why does the Apostles' Creed sometimes say that Jesus descended into Hell after His death on the Cross, and at other times that He descended to the dead?

A. To clarify the fact that Jesus did not descend to the Hell of the damned, but rather to the abode of the dead, or "lower regions" of the earth, where the souls of the just were waiting to be redeemed and taken to Heaven. According to the *Catechism of the Catholic Church* (cf. n. 633), the Bible calls the abode of the dead "hell," which is *Sheol* in Hebrew or *Hades* in Greek, because those who wind up there are deprived of the vision of God. This was true for all those people, whether evil or good, who had died before Jesus' redeeming death on the Cross.

Their state was not the same, however, as Jesus illustrated through the parable of the poor man Lazarus, who after death was received into "the bosom of Abraham," but remained separated by "a great chasm" from the rich man who had ignored his plight while they lived on earth (Luke 16:19-31). It was these just souls in Abraham's bosom (called the "spirits in prison" in 1 Peter 3:19) whom Jesus delivered when He descended into "Hell."

Q. What evidence can be cited to show that Jesus actually rose from the dead on Easter?

A. There are three strong pieces of evidence of the Resurrection: (1) the empty tomb, (2) the appearances to many disciples, and (3) the transformation of the Apostles.

First, the empty tomb. It is undisputed that the tomb in which Jesus was buried was empty on Easter morning. This fact was mentioned by all four Evangelists; by Mary Magdalene, and Peter and John; by the soldiers who had been guarding the tomb; and even by the enemies of Christ.

When the soldiers reported to the chief priests that they had witnessed an earthquake and the appearance of an angel, they were told not to spread that story, which was an admission that the tomb was empty. Instead, the chief priests paid the soldiers a large sum of money and instructed them to say that the Apostles had stolen the body of Christ while the soldiers were sleeping. They further promised that if the report of the soldiers sleeping on duty got back to Pontius Pilate, they would speak to him and keep the soldiers out of trouble (cf. Matthew 28:14).

There are several flaws in that explanation. The most obvious is that a sleeping person is in no position to witness anything. Second, Peter and John discovered the burial cloths still in the tomb. What person or persons trying to steal a body would take the time to remove the body from the large cloth and roll up the small cloth and place it to one side? And third, had the Apostles demonstrated the courage and daring that would have been necessary to steal the body from a heavily guarded tomb? On the contrary, these frightened and confused men were behind locked doors in the Upper Room, fearful that what happened to Jesus might also happen to them.

Second, Jesus was seen by hundreds of people after the Resurrection, first by Mary Magdalene and later by the holy women, the two disciples on the road to Emmaus, Simon Peter, ten of the Apostles on Easter night and eleven on the following Sunday, and, according to St. Paul, by a crowd of 500 (cf. 1 Corinthians 15:6). He talked with them, ate with them, showed them His wounds, and instructed them to "go, therefore, and make disciples of all nations, baptizing them in the name of the Father, and of the Son, and of the holy Spirit, teaching them to observe all that I have commanded you" (Matthew 28:19-20).

The usual objection to the appearances of Christ is that His disciples were hallucinating. Shattered by the death of Christ, the objection goes, they wanted to believe that He was alive and, over a period of time, convinced themselves that myth was reality. Now perhaps if Jesus had appeared only to a few people, and the appearances occurred, say, only at night, there might be some substance to this theory.

But that is not the way it happened. Some of the apparitions took place in Jerusalem, some in Galilee seventy miles away. They occurred in the morning, at noon, and at night, some out in the open, some behind closed doors. Jesus appeared to individuals, to small groups, and to a crowd of 500. To suggest that all of these people, in various places and at various times, were seeing things makes no sense. Furthermore, if all these people were crazy in thinking that they had seen Jesus, how come they all stopped being crazy exactly forty days after Easter? Since when do allegedly deluded minds act with such unanimity?

Third, only the bodily resurrection of Jesus can explain

the transformation of the Apostles from timid, frightened, and simple men to zealous, courageous, and articulate missionaries who, along with their disciples, converted the hostile Roman Empire to Christianity in less than 300 years. At first, they were terrified and thought that Jesus was a ghost (cf. Luke 24:37), and some even doubted up until the Ascension (cf. Matthew 28:17). But once convinced of the Resurrection, they preached the risen Christ openly and fearlessly, at the risk of their lives, something that they would never have done unless they truly believed that Jesus had overcome death.

The Apostles could have denied Christ and escaped torture and violent death, but none of them ever wavered. They preached the word of Christ, performed miracles in His name, and changed the course of human history. They offer the greatest testimony to Jesus' promise:

> "I am the resurrection and the life; whoever believes in me, even if he dies, will live, and everyone who lives and believes in me will never die" (John 11:25-26).

Q. What do we say to those who contend that the Resurrection of Jesus was not an historical event, but rather a spiritual happening, something outside the physical order?

A. We say that this is contrary to what the Catholic Church has taught for 2,000 years. In the words of the *Catechism of the Catholic Church:* "The mystery of Christ's Resurrection is a real event, with manifestations that were historically verified, as the New Testament bears witness" (n. 639). The *Catechism* cites as historical verification the following passage from 1 Corinthians 15:3-4:

> "I delivered to you as of first importance what I also received, that Christ died for our sins in accordance with the scriptures, and that he was buried, that he was raised

on the third day in accordance with the scriptures, and that he appeared to Cephas [Peter], then to the Twelve ...."

The *Catechism* goes on to say that "given all these testimonies, Christ's Resurrection cannot be interpreted as something outside the physical order, and it is impossible not to acknowledge it as an historical fact" (n. 643).

Q. How about those who say that the body of the risen Christ was not the same body that had been placed in the tomb?

A. It was the same body, but now in a glorified state. Referring to the body of the risen Christ, the *United States Catholic Catechism for Adults* (p. 95) says that "He was not a ghost; Jesus invited them to touch him. He asked for a piece of fish to show them that he could eat. He spent time with them, often repeating teachings from the days before the Passion but now in the light of the Resurrection. Nor was it a body like that of Lazarus, which would die again."

No, the *U.S. Catechism* continues, "his risen body would never die. Christ's body was glorified; it is not confined by space or time. He could appear and disappear before the Apostles' eyes. Closed doors did not bar his entry. It is a real body, but glorified, not belonging to earth but to the Father's realm. It is a body transformed by the Holy Spirit (cf. 1 Cor 15:42-44). The Holy Spirit 'gave life to Jesus' dead humanity and called it to the glorious state of Lordship' (CCC, n. 648)."

Q. Why didn't some of those who saw Jesus after the Resurrection recognize Him?

A. Perhaps because they did not expect to see Jesus. They were distraught over His death and thought that they would never see Him again. Perhaps because, as noted in the previous answer, He was not in a resuscitated state, as Lazarus had been, but rather in a glorified state. In other words, there was something different about Him. Or perhaps because He chose not to be recognized, to be visible or invisible, to be seen clearly by some but not by others. "Their eyes were prevented from recognizing him" (Luke 24:16), St. Luke says of the two disciples on the way to Emmaus, who later recognized the Lord "in the breaking of the bread" (Luke 24:35).

St. Peter told those in the house of Cornelius that God raised Jesus on the third day and "granted that he be visible, not to all the people, but to us, the witnesses chosen by God in advance, who ate and drank with him after he rose from the dead" (Acts 10:40-41).

Q. Why does the Creed say that Jesus rose "again" from the dead, as if He had risen once before?

A. Like many words, "again" can be understood in different ways. One common meaning, as the question implies, is that a certain action occurred at least once before and is now happening a second time. But that is not the meaning of "again" when we talk about the Resurrection, for Jesus rose from the dead only once, on the first Easter.

Another meaning of "again," according to *Webster's New World Dictionary*, is "back into a former position or condition [he is well again]." This is the correct understanding of the word as it appears in the Creed: Jesus died but is now alive again after rising from the dead.

Q. What about reports in the media that the bones of Jesus were found in a family tomb in a suburb of Jerusalem?

A. There is no credibility to these reports, which surfaced on TV's Discovery Channel in 2007. According to the reports, the remains were discovered in 1980 in an ossuary, or depository for bones, that bore an inscription which appeared to read, "Jesus, son of Joseph." We say "appeared to read" because the name on the ossuary was barely scratched on the limestone surface and is very difficult to decipher. This is puzzling because the inscriptions on the other ossuaries in the tomb were clearly readable.

The Israeli archaeologist who conducted the excavation in 1980 has rejected the claim that this was the tomb of Jesus of Nazareth, questioning whether the poorly scratched inscription even referred to Jesus in the first place and noting that the names of Jesus and Joseph were commonplace in first-century Palestine.

Apart from the fact that there is strong historical evidence that Jesus rose from the dead, as noted above, it is also odd that the family of Jesus would have a tomb in Jerusalem since they lived seventy miles away in Nazareth. Put this down as another weak attempt to undermine belief in Christ and in His Resurrection.

Chapter 9

Jesus and the Last Things

Q. The word "Purgatory" is not in the Bible, but did Jesus say anything about praying for the dead?

A. True, the word "Purgatory" is not in the Bible (and neither is the word "Trinity," for that matter), but the doctrine of prayers for the dead is taught in Holy Scripture. In 2nd Maccabees (12:45), for example, prayers for the dead are called a "holy and pious" thing. In the Book of Wisdom, there is a passage that we often hear at funeral Masses about the souls of the just being "in the hand of God,/ and no torment shall touch them .... Chastised a little, they shall be greatly blessed,/ because God tried them/ and found them worthy of himself" (Wisdom 3:1, 5). Purgatory is where we will be "chastised a little" for not doing enough in this life to make up for our sins.

In the New Testament, Jesus warns those who do not make peace with their neighbor, that they will be thrown into prison and that "you will not be released until you have paid the last penny" (Matthew 5:26 and Luke 12:59). The Church has seen these words of Christ as referring to the need for complete purification from all attachment to sin before we can enter Heaven.

Then there is Jesus' statement that "whoever speaks a word against the Son of Man will be forgiven; but whoever speaks against the holy Spirit will not be forgiven, either in this age or in the age to come" (Matthew 12:32). This implies that some sins, or the effects of sins that have already been forgiven, will be forgiven in the age to come. This can't mean Hell, where there is no possibility of forgiveness, or Heaven, where there is no need for forgiveness, so it must mean Purgatory, where we will not be released until we have paid the last penny.

There is also the passage where St. Paul talks about fire purifying gold and silver (our good works), while it burns away wood, hay, and straw (our imperfect works). When our lives are tested on the day of judgment, says Paul, each person "will receive a wage. But if someone's work is burned up, that one will suffer loss; the person will be saved, but only as through fire" (1 Corinthians 3:14-15).

The purgatorial fire will burn away all the impurities and imperfections that we have accumulated in this life and will prepare us for entry into the new and heavenly Jerusalem, where nothing unclean can enter (cf. Revelation 21:27).

Q. Did Jesus have much to say about Hell?

A. Jesus actually talked more about Hell than He did about Heaven, but He often used the word "Gehenna." This referred to a valley near Jerusalem that was a place of idol worship and human sacrifice and was considered to be a place of fire and punishment after death. In the Sermon on the Mount, for example, Jesus said that anyone who calls his brother a fool "will be liable to fiery Gehenna" (Matthew 5:22), and that it would be better to have one's eye gouged out or one's hand cut off than "to have your whole body thrown into Gehenna" (Matthew 5:29).

Our Lord referred to Gehenna as "unquenchable fire" (Mark 9:43) and as "the outer darkness, where there will be wailing and grinding of teeth" (Matthew 8:12), and said that at the end of the world, He will send His angels to round up all evildoers and "throw them into the fiery furnace, where there will be wailing and grinding of teeth" (Matthew 13:41-42).

In His description of the Last Judgment in chapter 25 of Matthew, Jesus issued this warning to those who did not help the least of His brothers and sisters: " 'Depart from me, you accursed, into the eternal fire prepared for the devil and his angels' " (25:41). " 'Amen, I say to you,' " said Christ, " 'what you did not do for one of these least ones, you did not do for me.' And these will go off to eternal punishment, but the righteous to eternal life" (25:45-46).

Q. How are we to understand Jesus' statements, as in Matthew 7:13-14, about the number of people who might wind up in Hell?

A. "Enter through the narrow gate; for the gate is wide and and the road broad that leads to destruction, and those who enter through it are many," Jesus said. "How narrow the gate and constricted the road that leads to life. And those who find it are few."

There has been much speculation about what Jesus meant by "many" and "few," but such speculation is foolish. Better for us to consider the affirmations about Hell in Scripture as a call to make use of our free will with a view to our eternal destiny and as an urgent call to conversion. Bear in mind that God predestines no one to go to Hell. For this to happen, there must be a willful turning away from Him and persistence in sin until the end.

God wants everyone to be saved (cf. 1 Timothy 2:4) and sends no one to Hell; people choose eternal damnation by the conscious choices they make in this life. Let us seek to make only those choices that are pleasing to God.

Q. Where did Christ say that He saw Satan fall from Heaven, and what was the reason for the fall?

A. In Luke 10:17-18, it says that the seventy-two disciples returned from a mission rejoicing and said that "even the demons are subject to us because of your name." Jesus said, "I have observed Satan fall like lightning from the sky."

Satan and the other demons were created good by God, but became evil by their own choice. Their fall from Heaven, says the *Catechism* (n. 392), "consists in the free choice of these created spirits, who radically and irrevocably *rejected* God and his reign." The *Catechism* (n. 393) goes on to say that "it is the *irrevocable* character of their choice, and not a defect in the infinite divine mercy, that makes the angels' sin unforgivable. 'There is no repentance for the angels after their fall, just as there is no repentance for men after death' " [St. John Damascene, *De Fide orth.* 2, 4: PG 94, 877].

As for the reason why Satan and his minions rebelled against God, the Vatican document *Christian Faith and Demonology* says that the majority of the early Church Fathers "saw the angels' pride as the reason for their fall. The 'pride' of the angels was manifested in their desire to exalt themselves above their condition, to maintain complete independence, and to make themselves divine. Many Fathers, however, emphasized not only the pride of the angels, but also their malice toward men. For St. Irenaeus, the Devil's apostasy began when he became jealous of man and sought to make him rebel against his Creator."

Q. In chapter 13 of Mark's Gospel (and chapters 24 of Matthew and 21 of Luke), Jesus speaks about the signs pointing to the end of the world, but then says that this generation will not pass away until all these things have taken place. Was He referring to the destruction of Jerusalem in A.D. 70 or to the end times or to both?

A. Jesus is speaking about both events - one imminent, the other at a day and hour that is known only to the Father. Many people think the signs point mostly to the end of the world, but this is not the view of David B. Currie, a former Fundamentalist missionary and former Rapture believer whose lifelong study of the Bible led him into the Catholic Church. Currie contends that all of the signs usually cited in connection with the end times actually came to pass within the generation of those who heard Jesus, and he explains his thesis in chapter six ("The Olivet Discourse") of his book entitled *Rapture*.

What is important to keep in mind, says Currie, is that Jesus was responding to two separate questions: (1) When will the destruction of the Temple happen? (Jesus had predicted that not one stone would be left upon another stone), and (2) What signs would indicate His Second Coming and the end of the world? (cf. Matthew 24:3).

Regarding the first question and relying on Matthew's account of the Olivet Discourse, Currie says that Jesus mentioned eight signs leading to the destruction of the Temple: the appearance of false messiahs (Matthew 24:4-5), wars and rumors of wars (24:6), famines and earthquakes (two separate signs) in various places (24:7), persecution and execution of Christians (24:9), apostasy from the faith and betrayal of one another (24:10-12), the gospel preached worldwide (24:14), and the "desolating abomination" (24:15) predicted by Daniel and fulfilled when the Roman armies surrounded Jerusalem.

Currie says that Jesus gave additional warnings to the early Church by providing five amplifications of the eight signs: the Great Tribulation (Matthew 24:21-22), the rise of false prophets teaching heresy (24:23-25), political upheaval (24:29), the signs in the heavens of the Son of Man (24:30-31), and the flowering of the fig tree (24:32-34).

While he explains in detail each of the five amplifications, Currie's discussion of the signs in the sky just before the fall of Jerusalem is particularly interesting. His source is the Jewish historian Josephus, who relied on eyewitness testimony for the following statements:

"There was a star resembling a sword, which stood over the city, and a comet, that continued a whole year .... Before the Jews' rebellion ... so great a light shone round the altar and the holy house, that it appeared to be bright daytime; which lasted for half an hour .... Moreover, the eastern gate of the inner court of the Temple ... was seen to be opened of its own accord about the sixth hour of the night .... The men of learning understood it, that *the security of their holy house was dissolved of its own accord* .... So these publicly declared that *the signal foreshadowed the desolation* that was coming upon them."

As for the second question about the end of the world, Currie contends that Jesus gave no signs pointing to when that might occur. All we know, he says, is that the second coming will be sudden and unexpected, like the flood in the days of Noah (24:37) or like lightning flashing from east to west (24:27). There will be no secret "rapture" when Christ comes again in all His glory. His coming will be very noticeable and accompanied by angels and trumpet blasts (24:31). That's why Jesus urges us over and over again to "be prepared, for at an hour you do not expect, the Son of Man will come" (24:44).

This is illustrated, says Currie, by three parables told by Christ (and explained by Currie): the faithful servant and the wicked servant (24:45-51), the wise and foolish virgins (25:1-13), and the distribution of the talents (25:14-30).

Such a brief summary of a chapter that is more than 50 pages long cannot do justice to the scholarship demonstrated by Mr. Currie. Those interested in his full explanation of these controversial passages should read the whole of chapter six, as well as the rest of his book.

Q. When will the Kingdom of God come?
A. The Kingdom has been here ever since Jesus proclaimed that "the kingdom of God is at hand" (Mark 1:15), but it will not reach its fullness until after the final judgment of the world. In his *Credo of the People of God*, Pope Paul VI said: "We confess that the kingdom of God begun here below in the Church of Christ is not of this world whose form is passing, and that its proper growth cannot be confounded with the progress of civilization, of science, or of human technology."

The Holy Father said that the kingdom "consists in an ever more profound knowledge of the unfathomable riches of Christ, an ever stronger hope in eternal blessings, an ever more ardent response to the love of God, and an ever more generous bestowal of grace and holiness among men."

Q. If God is a spirit and has no bodily parts, how can Jesus be seated as His right hand?

A. To be placed at the right hand of a king or ruler has always been considered a sign of high esteem and, in Jewish families, the honor of sitting "at the right hand of the father" was accorded to the oldest son. It is correct to say that God does not have a right hand; the expression is meant to signify that Jesus, as God's only Son, is equal to His Father and occupies the highest place in Heaven. In the words of St. John Damascene:

"By 'the Father's right hand' we understand the glory and honor of divinity, where he who exists as Son of God before all ages, indeed as God, of one being with the Father, is seated bodily after he became incarnate and his flesh was glorified" (*De Fide orth.*, 4, 2: PG 94, 1104C).

Whoever takes the Son gets everything!

AFTERWORD

There was a wealthy man who loved to collect rare works of art and, over the years, he had accumulated the works of many famous artists. He and his only son spent hours together discussing and admiring their treasures.

When war broke out in the Persian Gulf in 1991, the son joined the military and went off to fight in the war. He was very courageous and died in battle while rescuing another soldier. The father was notified of his son's death and grieved deeply.

Some months later, a young fellow came to the man's door carrying a large package. "You don't know me, sir," the fellow said, "but I am the soldier for whom your son gave his life. He was carrying me to safety when a bullet struck him in the heart."

The soldier went on to say that he and the man's son often spoke about the father's love for art. "I know this isn't much," he said, holding the package out to the father, "and I'm not a good artist, but I think your son would have wanted you to have this."

The father opened the package and was stunned to see a portrait of his son that the young man had painted. He stared in awe at the way the personality of his son had been captured, thanked the soldier profusely, and offered to pay him for the painting. "Oh, no, sir," the soldier said. "I could never repay what your son did for me. This is a gift."

The father hung the portrait over his mantel and, every time visitors came to his home, he showed them the painting of his son before taking them to see the great works of art he had collected over the years.

When the father died a few years later, there was an auction of his paintings. Many rich people gathered for the auction, excited over the opportunity to purchase some of the masterpieces on display. On the platform sat the soldier's portrait of the man's son and, when the auctioneer pounded the gavel, he said, "We will start the bidding on this picture of the son."

There was silence at first, but then someone said, "We want to see the famous paintings. Skip this one." But the auctioneer persisted and asked, "What will you bid for this painting of the son? Do I hear $200?" But there was no bid, only a man shouting, "We didn't come here to see that painting. Let's get to the real auction."

But the auctioneer continued, "The son, the son, who will take the son?" Finally, from the back of the room someone said, "I'll give $10 for that painting." It was the man's longtime gardener. He had little money, but he knew how much the father loved the son and the painting of him.

"We have $10," said the auctioneer. "Who will bid $20?" Another in the crowd yelled, "Give it to him for $10, and let's get to the masterpieces." The auctioneer replied, "$10 is the bid. Won't someone bid $20?" The crowd was becoming angry, so the auctioneer pounded his gavel again and said, "Going once, going twice, SOLD for $10."

A man in the second row said, "Good, now let's get to the real auction." But the auctioneer laid down his gavel and said, "I'm sorry, the auction is over. When I was called to conduct this auction, I was told of a secret provision in the owner's will that I could not reveal until now."

He said that the owner had stipulated that "only the painting of his son would be auctioned off and that whoever bought that painting would inherit all the other paintings. It was the owner's wish that the man who took the son would get everything."

The moral of the story is that God so loved the world that He gave His only Son, so that everyone who believes in Him might not perish, but might have eternal life. And it has been true for 2,000 years, that whoever takes the Son gets everything!

THE COMING OF THE MESSIAH

God sent prophets to prepare the way
For the Messiah who would come some day.

And then one night, after years of them,
Christ was born in Bethlehem.

He was God's Son, He was God's Word,
He spread God's love to all who heard.

He died for women, He died for men,
On Easter morn, He rose again.

He started a Church with Peter and Paul
And promised His Church would never fall.

If Jesus were here, this is what He'd say,
"Love God and others every single day.

"Confess your sins and grace will flood,
Be sure you eat my Body and Blood.

"And go to Church, make sure you pray,
You'll get to Heaven with little delay."

That's salvation history in words that rhyme,
About Jesus coming in the fullness of time.

CATHOLIC PRAYERS

Sign of the Cross

In the name of the Father,
and of the Son,
and of the Holy Spirit.
Amen.

In nomine Patris
et Filii,
et Spiritus Sancti.
Amen.

The Lord's Prayer

Our Father, who art in heaven,
hallowed be thy name;
thy kingdom come,
thy will be done on earth
as it is in heaven.
Give us this day our daily
bread, and forgive us our
trespasses as we forgive those
who trespass against us,
and lead us not into temptation,
but deliver us from evil.
Amen.

Pater noster, qui es in caelis,
sanctificetur nomen tuum;
adveniat regnum tuum;
fiat voluntas tua
sicut in caelo, et in terra.
Panem nostrum quotidianum
da nobis hodie,
et dimitte nobis debita nostra,
sicut et nos dimittimus
debitoribus nostris et ne nos
in ducas in tentationem
sed libera nos a malo.
Amen.

The Hail Mary

Hail Mary, full of grace,
the Lord is with thee.
Blessed art thou among
women, and blessed is the
fruit of thy womb, Jesus.
Holy Mary, Mother of God,
pray for us sinners now and
at the hour of our death.
Amen.

Ave, Maria, gratia plena,
Dominus tecum.
Benedicta tu in mulieribus
et benedictus fructus
ventris tui, Iesus.
Sancta Maria, Mater Dei,
ora pro nobis peccatoribus,
nunc et in hora mortis nostrae.
Amen.

Glory Be to the Father

Glory be to the Father,
and to the Son,
and to the Holy Spirit.
As it was in the beginning,
is now, and ever shall be,
world without end.
Amen.

Gloria Patri, et Filio,
et Spiritui Sancto.
Sicut erat in principio,
et nunc, et semper,
et in saecula saeculorum.
Amen.

Hail, Holy Queen

Hail, Holy Queen, Mother of
Mercy, our life, our sweetness,
and our hope. To thee do we
cry, poor banished children
of Eve. To thee do we send
up our sighs, mourning and
weeping in this valley of tears.
Turn then, most gracious
advocate, thine eyes of mercy
toward us, and after this our
exile, show unto us the blessed
fruit of thy womb, Jesus.
O clement, O loving,
O sweet Virgin Mary,
pray for us, O holy Mother
of God, that we may be made
worthy of the promises of Christ.
Amen.

Salve, Regina, mater-
misericordiae, vita, dulcedo et
spes nostra, salve. Ad te
clamamus, exsules filii Evae.
Ad te suspiramus gementes et
flentes in hac lacrimarum valle.
Eia ergo, advocata nostra,
illos tuos misericordes oculos
ad nos converte et Iesum,
benedictum fructum ventris tui,
nobis post hoc exsilium ostende.
O clemens, O pia, O dulcis
Virgo Maria!
Ora pro nobis,
sancta Dei Genetrix.
Ut digni efficiamur
promissionibus Christi.
Amen.

The Apostles' Creed

I believe in God,
the Father almighty,
Creator of heaven and earth.
I believe in Jesus Christ,
his only Son, our Lord.
He was conceived by the
power of the Holy Spirit,
born of the Virgin Mary,
suffered under Pontius Pilate,

Credo in Deum, Patrem
omnipotentem, Creatorem
caeli et terrae; et in Iesum
Christum, Filium eius unicum,
Dominum nostrum, qui
conceptus est de Spiritu Sancto,
natus ex Maria Virgine, passus
sub Pontio Pilato, crucifixus,
mortuus, et sepultus. Descendit

was crucified, died, and was buried. He descended into hell. On the third day he rose again. He ascended into heaven and is seated at the right hand of the Father. He will come again to judge the living and the dead. I believe in the Holy Spirit, the holy catholic church, the communion of saints, the forgiveness of sins, the resurrection of the body, and life everlasting. Amen.

ad inferos; tertia die resurrexit a mortuis, ascendit ad caelos, sedet ad dexteram Dei, Patris omnipotentis in de venturus est judicare vivos et mortuos. Credo in Spiritum Sanctum, sanctam ecclesiam catholicam, sanctorum communionem, remissionem peccatorum, carnis resurrexionem, vitam aeternam. Amen.

The Mysteries of the Rosary

The Joyful Mysteries (Monday and Saturday)
The Annunciation by the Angel to Mary
The Visitation of Mary to Elizabeth
The Birth of Our Lord in Bethlehem
The Presentation of Jesus in the Temple
The Finding of the Child Jesus in the Temple

The Luminous Mysteries (Thursday)
The Baptism of Jesus in the Jordan
The Miracle of the Wine at Cana
The Proclamation of the Kingdom
The Transfiguration of Jesus
The Institution of the Eucharist

The Sorrowful Mysteries (Tuesday and Friday)
The Agony in the Garden
The Scourging at the Pillar
The Crowning with Thorns
The Carrying of the Cross
The Crucifixion and Death of Our Lord

The Glorious Mysteries (Sunday and Wednesday)
The Resurrection of Jesus from the Dead
The Ascension of Jesus into Heaven
The Descent of the Holy Spirit on the Apostles
The Assumption of Mary into Heaven
The Crowning of Mary as Queen of Heaven and Earth

How to Pray the Rosary

Make the Sign of the Cross and, while holding the crucifix, say the Apostles' Creed. On the first bead, say an Our Father, Hail Marys on the next three beads, and a Glory Be on the last bead. For each of the five decades on the main part of the rosary, announce the mystery, say an Our Father and then ten Hail Marys while fingering each bead and meditating on the mystery.

Finish each decade with a Glory Be and the prayer requested by Our Lady of Fatima ("O my Jesus, forgive us our sins, save us from the fires of hell, lead all souls to heaven, especially those who have the most need of your mercy.").

After the five decades, say the Hail Holy Queen and, before making the Sign of the Cross, say: "O God, whose only begotten Son, by His life, Death, and Resurrection, has purchased for us the rewards of eternal life, grant, we beseech Thee, that by meditating on these mysteries of the most holy rosary of the Blessed Virgin Mary, we may imitate what they contain and obtain what they promise, through the same Christ our Lord. Amen."

Stations of the Cross

While standing before each station, say while genuflecting, "We adore you, O Christ, and we praise you, because by your holy Cross you have redeemed the world." Then say an Our Father, a Hail Mary, and a Glory Be to the Father while meditating on the particular event during the Passion and Death of our Lord.

First Station:	Jesus is condemned to death by Pontius Pilate.
Second Station:	Jesus carries His Cross.
Third Station:	Jesus falls the first time.
Fourth Station:	Jesus meets His sorrowful mother.
Fifth Station:	Simon of Cyrene helps Jesus to carry His Cross.
Sixth Station:	Veronica wipes the face of Jesus.
Seventh Station:	Jesus falls the second time.
Eighth Station:	Jesus meets the women of Jerusalem.
Ninth Station:	Jesus falls a third time.
Tenth Station:	Jesus is stripped of His clothes.
Eleventh Station:	Jesus is nailed to the Cross.
Twelfth Station:	Jesus dies on the Cross.
Thirteenth Station:	Jesus is taken down from the Cross.
Fourteenth Station:	The body of Jesus is laid in the tomb.

Act of Contrition *(Traditional Version)*

O my God, I am heartily sorry for having offended Thee, and I detest all my sins because I dread the loss of heaven and the pains of hell, but most of all because they have offended Thee, my God, who art all good and deserving of all my love. I firmly resolve, with the help of thy grace, to confess my sins, to do penance, and to amend my life. Amen.

Act of Contrition *(Alternate Version)*

O my God, I am sorry for my sins with all my heart. In choosing to do wrong and failing to do good, I have sinned against You whom I should love above all things. I firmly intend, with your help, to do penance, to sin no more, and to avoid whatever leads me to sin.
Amen.

Act of Contrition *(Alternate Version)*

Lord Jesus, Son of God, have mercy on me, a sinner.

The Divine Praises

Blessed be God.
Blessed be His Holy Name.
Blessed be Jesus Christ, true God and true Man.
Blessed be the Name of Jesus.
Blessed be His most Sacred Heart.
Blessed be His most Precious Blood.
Blessed be Jesus in the most Holy Sacrament of the Altar.
Blessed be the Holy Spirit, the Paraclete.
Blessed be the great Mother of God, Mary most holy.
Blessed be her holy and Immaculate Conception.
Blessed be her glorious Assumption.
Blessed be the name of Mary, Virgin and Mother.
Blessed be St. Joseph, her most chaste spouse.
Blessed be God in His angels and in His saints.

BIBLIOGRAPHY

Benedict XVI, Pope. *Jesus of Nazareth*
_____. *Jesus, the Apostles, and the Early Church*

Catechism of the Catholic Church
Catholic Answers. *The Essential Catholic Survival Guide*
Compendium of the Catechism of the Catholic Church
Currie, David B. *Rapture*

Documents of Vatican II. Edited by Walter M. Abbott, S.J.
Drummey, James J. *Catholic Replies*
_____. *Catholic Replies 2*

Gray, Tim. *Mission of the Messiah*

Hayes, Fr. Edward J., Hayes, Msgr. Paul J., and Drummey,
    James J. *Catholicism and Reason*
_____. *Catholicism and Scripture*

John Paul II, Pope. *Mother of the Redeemer*
_____. *The Splendor of Truth*

McKenzie, John L., S.J. *Dictionary of the Bible*

Ray, Stephen K. *St. John's Gospel*
Ricciotti, Giuseppe, *Life of Christ*
Rumble, Rev. Dr. Leslie, and Carty, Rev. Charles M.
    Radio Replies (3 Vols.)

Sheed, Frank. *To Know Christ Jesus*
Sheen, Fulton J. *Life of Christ*

United States Catholic Catechism for Adults

INDEX